Trauma-Informed Teaching and IEPs

Trauma-Informed Teaching and IEPs

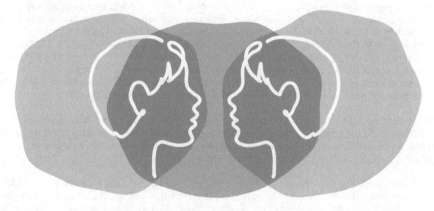

Strategies for Building Student Resilience

MELISSA SADIN

ascd

Arlington, Virginia USA

2800 Shirlington Road, Suite 1001 • Arlington, VA 22206 USA
Phone: 1-800-933-2723 or 1-703-578-9600 • Fax: 1-703-575-5400
Website: www.ascd.org • Email: member@ascd.org
Author guidelines: www.ascd.org/write

Penny Reinart, *Chief Impact Officer*; Genny Ostertag, *Managing Director, Book Acquisitions & Editing*; Susan Hills, *Senior Acquisitions Editor*; Julie Houtz, *Director, Book Editing*; Mary Beth Nielsen, *Editor*; Thomas Lytle, *Creative Director*; Donald Ely, *Art Director*; Georgia Park, *Senior Graphic Designer*; Keith Demmons, *Production Designer*; Kelly Marshall, *Production Manager*; Shajuan Martin, *E-Publishing Specialist*

PAPERBACK ISBN: 978-1-4166-3127-9   ASCD product #122026   n8/22
PDF E-BOOK ISBN: 978-1-4166-3128-6; see Books in Print for other formats.

Quantity discounts are available: email programteam@ascd.org or call 1-800-933-2723, ext. 5773, or 1-703-575-5773. For desk copies, go to www.ascd.org/deskcopy.

Library of Congress Cataloging-in-Publication Data
Names: Sadin, Melissa, author.
Title: Trauma-informed teaching and IEPs : strategies for building student resilience / Melissa Sadin.
Description: Arlington, Virginia : ASCD, 2022. | Includes bibliographical references and index.
Identifiers: LCCN 2022017376 (print) | LCCN 2022017377 (ebook) | ISBN 9781416631279 (paperback) | ISBN 9781416631286 (pdf)
Subjects: LCSH: Children with mental disabilities--Education. | Psychic trauma in children. | Post-traumatic stress disorder in children. | Individualized education programs.
Classification: LCC LC4601 .S24 2022 (print) | LCC LC4601 (ebook) | DDC 371.92--dc23/eng/20220608
LC record available at https://lccn.loc.gov/2022017376
LC ebook record available at https://lccn.loc.gov/2022017377

31 30 29 28 27 26 25 24 23 22   1 2 3 4 5 6 7 8 9 10 11 12

This book is dedicated to my son, Noah, who taught me that even the quiet, academically able, and "well-behaved" children need special care. You are my life's joy and will always be special to me.

Trauma-Informed Teaching and IEPs

Strategies for Building Student Resilience

Introduction

Thank you—on behalf of all of your past, present, and future students, in general and special education—for reading this book. We, in education, have a problem, and that problem is twofold: (1) childhood trauma is a national health crisis—as many as two out of every three children in any classroom across the country have experienced some form of trauma (Duke et al., 2010); and (2) many of the students classified to receive special education are disproportionately children who have experienced trauma or are children of color (Blodgett, 2015). Some children who experience prolonged trauma have been shown to develop difficulties with behavior and learning (Lovallo, 2013).

The latest in brain research shows early exposure to traumatic situations (e.g., abuse, neglect, family violence, substance abuse in the home, discrimination) has a significant effect on brain development and the ability to learn. The research connects this change in brain development to language development, memory, processing speed, and emotional regulation. A connection also exists between exposure to early childhood trauma and children who receive special education services in our schools. A recent study in Washington State (Blodgett, 2015) showed that 80 percent of the children eligible for special education were exposed to early childhood trauma, which has been linked to dyslexia, attention deficit hyperactivity disorder (ADHD), emotional and behavioral disorders, and autism spectrum disorder. The same study showed Black children are four times more likely to be classified with intellectual disabilities and five times more likely than white students to be classified with an emotional or behavioral disorder.

Trauma and Disproportionality

A form of double jeopardy is at work here. In addition to being referred for eligibility for special education services, children who were exposed to adverse childhood experiences (ACEs), children receiving special education services, and children of color are all up to five times more likely to be a part of the school-to-prison pipeline (Kunjufu, 2005), which refers to the statistical evidence that children who are suspended are more likely to be involved with the juvenile or adult justice system (American Psychological Association Zero Tolerance Task Force, 2008). The school-to-prison pipeline grew out of the country's collective response to the shooting at Columbine High School. That was the beginning of our understanding that our schools might not be as safe as we thought they were. The spirit of a zero-tolerance policy was that schools were safe places for children who wanted to learn. If a student demonstrated unsafe behavior or brought weapons or drugs to school, they could be removed from the school. Teachers were scared. Parents and caregivers wanted assurances that their children were safe in school. School leaders wanted policy they could use to help create safe schools.

Over time, however, the zero-tolerance policies led to more and more school suspensions. Children were being expelled in record numbers. Some district leaders expanded the zero-tolerance policies to include repeat behaviors such as cursing or disrespect toward teachers. A few years after the nationwide implementation of zero-tolerance, researchers began to look at the impact of these practices on students. What they found was that Black and Hispanic students and male students who receive special education services were being suspended much more often than their nonminority and general education classmates (Balfanz et al., 2014). This practice is now referred to as *disproportionality*. Many states have an administrative code that attempts to thwart the practice of disproportionately suspending minority and special education students through careful reporting of discipline records. It is a start. We have a long way to go.

In addition, the research showed that minority students were suspended for nonviolent behaviors where nonminority students demonstrating the same behavior were only reprimanded (Skiba et al., 2014). The same longitudinal study showed that children who were suspended once in their freshman year were more likely to be suspended again. In addition, children who were suspended were more likely to have poor attendance. They were more likely to fail a class and a grade. They were more likely to drop out.

An in-depth review of the literature regarding the school-to-prison pipeline along with consideration of children with adverse childhood experiences in our schools expands disproportionality to include children with early childhood trauma. A review of school data in Washington State (Blodgett, 2015) showed that children with three or more ACEs were more likely to receive special education and fail a grade, and they were more likely to have poor attendance and more likely to drop out than their classmates with no ACEs. The children in the school-to-prison pipeline *are* the children with early childhood trauma. These are the children most likely to have been emotionally abandoned by their caregivers or their communities. They are our most vulnerable children, and they need our help.

Breaking the Cycle

Do you see the vicious cycle at work here? Children exposed to early childhood trauma and children of color are more likely to be found eligible for special education. Children exposed to early childhood trauma, children receiving special education, and children of color are all more likely to be suspended and excluded than general education white students. Children excluded and suspended are more likely to fail a grade, drop out, and become involved in the juvenile justice system. The common denominator is special education. And how do children get into special education? Through a rigorous evaluation process conducted by a team of experts trained to administer standardized tests and evaluate the results.

In some states this team comprises the child's parents, a school social worker, a school psychologist, relevant teachers, and possibly an administrator. Some states include a learning disabilities teacher consultant. This team has many names. In this book, as a tribute to the state of New Jersey where I dedicated most of my years as a teacher and administrator, we will call this team the child study team (CST). The CST is the lynchpin. For those who are members of this important group, this book dedicates an entire chapter to the development of trauma-informed and culturally competent individualized education programs (IEPs). If we can conduct evaluations and develop programs for children with an understanding of the effects of early childhood trauma on learning and behavior, we can reduce the number of children receiving special education services, keep more children in school, and disrupt the school-to-prison pipeline.

Goal

Currently, students receiving special education services may compose as much as 50 percent of our school populations. It is common to have anywhere from 1 to 100 percent of the children in any classroom receiving special education services (Losen et al., 2015). However, disproportionality and over-identification for special education are not just CST concerns. These students are in music classes, art classes, physical education, and extracurricular activities, and often, they are the children not making adequate yearly progress. This is a problem for all of us—for general education and special education teachers, counselors, evaluation teams, and administrators. This is a whole school problem and requires a whole school solution. Thus, all educators should learn how trauma affects the brain and how the resulting atypical neurological and psychological development affects learning and behavior. In this book, we will explore strategies for supporting our most vulnerable students that you can implement in general education settings, special education settings, across grade levels, and across the curriculum.

In most learning environments, children have received all that they need for typical neurological and psychological development. These students still come in many shapes and sizes—some have autism spectrum disorder, some have dyslexia, and some are gifted—but nationally, we know what's needed to provide an adequate education for these students. The challenge is with children who may not be getting the consistent care that they need or who are being harmed by the people who should be caring for them. These students need our unique consideration. They may have brains that are developing differently than children who get what they need from their primary caregivers. Thus, they need us to understand their development and provide strategies to meet their needs.

As educators, we all need to shift our paradigm. We need to shift our perspective—the way we see students. All students are not the same. They learn differently, see the world differently, and need different things for survival. Most of us have attended colleges and universities to learn to teach general education, special education, or both. Much of the current curriculum in preservice teaching programs is based on social learning theory. Many schools of social work have made great strides in preparing school social workers to work with children who have experienced trauma. School psychology programs are coming along, and some colleges and universities have made small inroads in changing their curriculum to support the research on developmental trauma (DT), but preservice teaching lags behind.

Social learning theory proposes that individuals learn by observing the behaviors of others. They then evaluate the effects of those behaviors by observing the positive and negative consequences that follow. This theory was constructed before researchers had the ability to study the limbic system, the autonomic nervous system, and its response to trauma. When a child does not get their basic needs met, the part of the brain that allows for observation and evaluation experiences a delay in development. The good news is that we do not need to throw away all that we have learned about child development and learning. We just need to expand our understanding of traumatology and add it to our repertoire. This book will cover the traumatology research and how it affects student learning and behavior. Once you understand the effects of trauma on learning and development, we will explore classroom strategies and IEP goals and modifications that can actually help to heal your students.

The Paradigm Shift

The paradigm shift to trauma-infomed practice requires you to change your thinking about students from "What is wrong with you?" to "What has happened to you?" It means leading with relationship building and making personal connections. The best news is that children without trauma respond just as well to personal connections and acceptance as children with trauma, so you can implement the strategies and approaches of this book in any class without disruption or calling attention to any specific students. If you treat all of your students as though they need acceptance and personal connections, you can help to heal the part of the brain that trauma delays, and your students will have better learning and behavioral outcomes.

We can replace that vicious cycle that results in students falling by the wayside with a healing one. General educators can shift their paradigm and implement the strategies outlined in this book to improve academic performance and decrease the number of students referred for special education services. Special educators shift their paradigm and implement strategies both in their inclusion classrooms and their replacement and full-day programs that will improve behavior and academic outcomes and, in some cases, return children to general education settings. CSTs may apply their shift in perspective to administration of the tests, to the analysis of the results, and to the development of trauma-informed and culturally competent IEPs that their general and special education colleagues will be prepared to implement.

Anyone who works in a school in the service of children needs to understand the prevalence of early childhood trauma and its effect on learning and behavior. Trauma-informed, culturally competent programs and practices have a profound positive influence on the achievement of our students who face the most challenges. These programs enhance the achievement of all of our students. You are reading this book; you are already a part of the solution.

1

Adverse Childhood Experiences and Their Effects on Development

The study that completely changed our understanding of the prevalence of childhood trauma was originally conducted more than a decade ago by Robert Anda, Vincent Felitti, and their team (Anda et al., 2010). The survey they administered to 17,000 college-educated participants was called the Adverse Childhood Experiences (ACEs) Survey. They asked each participant 10 questions about their childhood. Each time a participant replied "yes" to a question was counted as an ACE. Sixty-four percent of the participants replied "yes" to at least one adverse childhood experience. The results of this study demonstrated the overwhelming prevalence of childhood trauma. Further study illustrated that the number of ACEs an individual reports can clearly predict negative adult health outcomes. Adults who report three or more ACEs as children also report a significant increase in heart disease, cancer, mental illness, and substance abuse (Anda et al., 2010).

ACEs Expanded

Continued research in the field of ACEs has expanded our understanding of childhood adverse experiences. The original study listed 10 ACEs, but there are truly an unlimited number. In 2020, PACEs Connection highlighted three realms of ACEs: household, community, and environment. **Household** ACEs comprise the original 10—basically anything that takes place inside the home or school, including substance abuse, violence, aggression toward children, neglect, separation, and bullying.

The second realm of ACEs, **community**, can be considered the root cause of the first realm. Community ACEs include limited access to quality health care, racism, lack of access to proper nutrition, limited access to quality schools, and historical trauma. This realm illustrates the intersection where an understanding of trauma meets an understanding of cultural competence. It includes historical and intergenerational trauma. *Historical trauma* is trauma experienced by an ethnic or cultural group that has been enslaved, disenfranchised, interned, or impoverished. This type of trauma affects the gene pool and can influence children in generations yet to come.

Intergenerational trauma occurs when families experience the same or similar adverse experiences over generations. An example of intergenerational trauma is intergenerational poverty. Families living below the poverty line for multiple generations has a similar effect on the gene pool, with negative influences on health and financial security in future generations. The systemic racism and discrimination experienced by Black Americans is an example of intergenerational and historical trauma. Black children are born in this country every day bearing the scars of previous generations. These scars affect the development of the autonomic nervous system and the limbic system and the overall health and well-being of our Black students.

The third realm of ACEs is the **environment** and includes, but is not limited to, hurricanes, tornadoes, flooding, mudslides, and pandemics. A child who goes through an environmental event that threatens shelter security or food security, threatens the lives of self or family members, or otherwise affects the child's daily household function can be said to have had an adverse experience. The child who survives a tornado but loses her home or a family member has experienced trauma. This third realm provides us with an opportunity to recognize that trauma might not be anyone's fault. Childhood trauma is not just something that is done to a child by someone else; it can be something the child experiences that no one can prevent, like a hurricane or a tornado.

Know Your Own Experiences

The ACEs survey is a tool for adults to use—educators, parents, and CST members. All adults should know their own ACE score (Anda et al., 2010), especially those who work with children. If you have four or more ACEs, you may be experiencing some of the adult health outcomes, such as autoimmune weakness, intestinal distress, mental health challenges, heart disease, even cancer. Find a doctor who either knows about ACEs or is willing to learn. Anda and company believed that what's predictable is preventable. When you know what has happened to you, you can better advocate for your own healing. In addition, knowing what has happened to you will have a profound effect on how you see your students. You may find you have more empathy and compassion. You may find that you now understand why students affect you in different ways, whether positive or negative.

The first and most important step in becoming a trauma-informed, culturally competent educator is realizing your own culture and exposure to adverse childhood experiences. Identifying your own ACEs requires that you take an ACEs survey (see Figure 1.1). The original survey was designed for a homogeneous group of white middle-class, college-educated participants. That sample does not reflect all Americans. Experiencing discrimination in childhood because of your religion, race, culture, gender identity, or sexual orientation is also considered an ACE (Lanier, 2020). At the time of this writing, researchers are working to create more culturally appropriate survey questions. For now, take the survey in Figure 1.1 and add another "yes" if you feel that you have been exposed to or witnessed discrimination, bias, or racism.

FIGURE 1.1
Adverse Childhood Experiences Survey

Prior to your 18th birthday:

1. Did a parent or other adult in the household often or very often . . .
   Swear at you, insult you, put you down, or humiliate you?
   Act in a way that made you afraid that you might be physically hurt?

   No ___ If Yes, enter 1 ___

2. Did a parent or other adult in the household often or very often . . .
   Push, grab, slap, or throw something at you?
   Ever hit you so hard that you had marks or were injured?

   No ___ If Yes, enter 1 ___

3. Did an adult or person at least 5 years older than you ever . . .
   Touch or fondle you or have you touch their body in a sexual way?
   Attempt or actually have oral, anal, or vaginal intercourse with you?

   No ___ If Yes, enter 1 ___

4. Did you often or very often feel that . . .
   No one in your family loved you or thought you were important or special?
   Your family didn't look out for each other, feel close to each other, or support each other?

   No ___ If Yes, enter 1 ___

5. Did you often or very often feel that . . .
   You didn't have enough to eat, had to wear dirty clothes, and had no one to protect you?
   Your parents were too drunk or high to take care of you or take you to the doctor if
     you needed it?

   No ___ If Yes, enter 1 ___

6. Were your parents ever separated or divorced?

   No ___ If Yes, enter 1 ___

7. Was your mother or stepmother . . .
   Often or very often pushed, grabbed, slapped, or had something thrown at her?
   Sometimes, often, or very often kicked, bitten, hit with a fist, or hit with something hard?
   Ever repeatedly hit over at least a few minutes or threatened with a gun or knife?

   No ___ If Yes, enter 1 ___

8. Did you live with anyone who was a problem drinker or alcoholic, or who used street drugs?

   No ___ If Yes, enter 1 ___

9. Was a household member depressed or mentally ill, or did a household member attempt suicide?

   No ___ If Yes, enter 1 ___

10. Did a household member go to prison?

No ___ If Yes, enter 1 ___

Now add up your "Yes" answers: ____

This is your ACE score.

Source: Adapted from From "What ACEs/PCEs do you have?" by J. Stevens, May 2012, *ACEs Too High News.* https://acestoohigh.com/got-your-ace-score/.

Count your "yes" responses. If you find that you have more than three ACEs, you can take action that will improve your overall mental and physical health outcomes. Take action that seems right for you. If you struggle with trust and often struggle in relationships, perhaps trauma-informed therapy is right for you. If you have ongoing cardiac concerns or digestive tract issues, perhaps finding a medical doctor who is familiar with ACEs is right for you. Everyone who works in a school should know their ACE score.

That said, we are all more than our ACE scores. We are the result of both our adverse and positive childhood experiences. Resilience is the ability to adapt to change and overcome challenges. Research shows that people with high ACE scores and high resilience scores have more positive health outcomes than people with high ACE scores and low resilience scores (Sege & Brown, 2017). I strongly encourage you to consider your resilience score as well as your ACE score. You can find an adult resilience survey at www.originstraining.org. Devereux Advanced Behavioral Health's Center for Resilient Children also has one at www.centerforresilientchildren.org (Mackrain, 2013). (I'll cover building resilience in our students further in Chapter 3.)

Explore your culture. Who are you? Where do you come from? What were the morals and values you were raised to believe? Do these things shape the way you see others? The way you see students of different races or religions? We all carry with us an invisible backpack. All of our experiences, from conception and on through our lives, get added to this invisible backpack. You need to dig around in that backpack and identify the things that you were taught as a child and how those things affect your expectations for your colleagues and your students. If you are a white person, consider getting in touch with your white privilege. The best way I have found to do this is through reading and attending webinars on the topic. No matter your background, you should find an opportunity to speak with others. Ask different people questions about their perspectives. Learn about other cultures and religions. Come to understand child-rearing practices of people who are not the same as you. Everyone who works in a school should have the opportunity to learn about their own culture and the cultures of the adults and students in their school community. Coming to terms with your childhood trauma exposure and the contents of your invisible backpack will help you as you shift your paradigm.

Keep in mind that you should not administer the ACEs survey in school. Trauma happens when children endure a hardship over which they have no control. Children living in poverty cannot change their parents' ability to make money. Children cannot stop a parent's substance abuse. They cannot prevent a pandemic. Giving children the ACEs Survey can traumatize them; it is asking them to score all the things over which they have no control. In some individual circumstances at the high school level, it might be appropriate to administer an ACEs Survey to an upper-class student. Consider the emotional age of the student. Is the student about to launch into their own living space and a job or career? Does a counselor, school psychologist, or social worker know the student and have a good relationship? Then, it might be safe to conduct the survey with that student. Ultimately, however, we simply do not need to know the ACE score of all our students, so it shouldn't be rolled out to everyone.

So how can we use ACEs in schools? By making sure that all the adults in the school community understand the healing power of knowing your own ACE score. Teachers might be able to informally guess at student ACE scores and have more compassion for their students. Parents may come into the school and share with the CST or a counselor that their child has six ACEs. Knowing about ACEs gives them the ability to tell you that their child is experiencing trauma without having to divulge the details of the trauma. They preserve some privacy but can still get help for their children. CSTs can use ACEs while taking a social history and also during their initial data collection when a student is referred. This will be explained in greater detail in Chapter 4.

It is important, however, to recognize that an ACE for one child might not be an ACE for another. An example of this is our recent pandemic and subsequent lockdowns. When determining whether a child has experienced a trauma, one must consider the presence of protective factors. Consider Jawon,* a 7-year-old boy who lives with his mother, father, and older brother. Jawon's mother is a teacher, and his father is in construction. His parents keep their jobs through the pandemic. Jawon maintains his food and shelter security. Although he misses his friends at school and playing baseball, he can talk about it with his older brother. Jawon's basic needs continue to be met. Although the pandemic is life changing, Jawon has protective factors that mitigate the effect of those life changing events.

Now, consider Lily, a 6-year-old girl who lives with her mother. Lily's mother works three jobs to make ends meet. When the pandemic hits, the bar where she works closes, and she loses her job. Lily sometimes goes without meals. Lily is no longer able to go to school to see her friends. Finally, her mom finds another job but must work long hours. Lily is often home alone. The long hours separated from her mother, the fear she may have from being alone, the lack of food security, and the lack of protective factors would all contribute to the pandemic being an adverse childhood experience for Lily.

Trauma and Neurological Development

Part of being a trauma-aware educator is understanding the effects of trauma on children's neurological development. Children who

---

* All student and teacher names are pseudonyms.

endure adverse childhood experiences have brains that develop differently than children who are not exposed to trauma. Children who have three or more ACEs may have developmental trauma (DT), and repeated or chronic trauma exposure may impair neurobiological development. Childhood trauma causes atypical development of the amygdala, hippocampus, and prefrontal cortex. These important parts of our limbic system are necessary for, among other things, emotional control, language development, memory, and cognition (van der Kolk, 2005).

When we are born, our amygdala and autonomic nervous system (ANS) are fully operational. That is our survival brain. Our ANS comprises the parasympathetic system, which includes the vagus nerve and helps us inhibit stress and calm down, and the sympathetic nervous system, which gets us moving. These systems work together to provide balance in the nervous system, but more than that, recent research suggests that the ANS is a hierarchical system where newer circuits can inhibit or enhance older circuits (Porges & Carter, 2017). We humans are social beings. We need one another for survival. Human infants cannot feed themselves, keep themselves warm, or soothe themselves. They need other humans to survive. When infants are hungry, they cry. That is the ANS signaling that the baby needs food. The cry brings a parent or caregiver, and the baby's food or other basic needs are met. Calm is restored. This cycle of alarm and care is repeated thousands of times during the early childhood years. Each time the baby's needs are met, the ANS builds new circuits that establish regulation of the system, and the hippocampus is engaged. Mirror neurons in the brain learn to mimic the care being provided by the baby's family. Over time, the hippocampus develops the ability for the baby to regulate the alarm (Rosenthal et al., 1981).

For example, a 1-year-old child who is beginning to learn to walk will occasionally fall down. When she falls down, she might cry. Hearing the baby cry, a family member or caregiver comes over, picks the baby up, and soothes her in some way. Five years down the road, this same child is running outside with her friends. She falls down. She may breathe deeply. She may appear initially shocked. But she is also assessing herself for damage. The ANS is engaged. But the hippocampus is also engaged. The hippocampus is what allows her to scan herself for injury. In the absence of a scraped knee or a little blood on her hands, she may dust herself off, pick herself up, and continue to play with her friends. If she is truly injured, she may cry. It's the pause button between the fall and the crying that indicates that the hippocampus is growing in a typical fashion and assisting this child in her ability to regulate her emotions. Thus, children whose needs are consistently met, who are not exposed to childhood trauma, have emotional regulation that is consistent with their chronological age.

needs met not exposed to trauma have emotional regulation

For some children, the cycle of care is not consistent. The attention of a caregiver or a parent may be inconsistent as a result of poverty, substance abuse, violence in the home or community, or maltreatment. In this case, the child's basic needs are not met. A child cries because he is hungry. No one comes or the caregiver comes inconsistently. The amygdala remains on high alert. When the amygdala remains on high alert, often over the course of years, the hippocampus development is delayed. In some cases, the amygdala can grow and become larger than it would be in the case of a child whose needs are consistently met (Hanson et al., 2014). A child whose ANS fires often as a result of unmet needs or maltreatment and whose hippocampal development is delayed often does not have emotional regulation that is consistent with their chronological age. Those new circuits that should be created through the soothing and consistent care of others do not develop appropriately.

hippocampus delayed growth when needs not met

needs not met often do not have emot. regulation

The ANS is also linked to the hypothalamic-pituitary adrenocortical axis or the stress response system (Tottenham & Sheridan, 2010). This system is an important mediator of stressful experiences for humans. The ANS is affected by large amounts of cortisol and adrenaline production (Alink et al., 2012).

cortisol adrenaline

Consider that there are three types of stress: positive, tolerable, and toxic (see Figure 1.2). **Positive stress** is an important part of brain development. For example, imagine that Julio, an 8-year-old boy, has a goldfish that he keeps in a bowl in his bedroom. One day Julio looks at his goldfish and finds that Goldie is floating on the top of the water. He takes his goldfish bowl, and he walks into the kitchen where his mother is cooking and says, "Mom, there's something wrong with Goldie." Julio's mom takes a look at the fish and explains to Julio that Goldie has passed away. Julio is understandably upset. Maybe he even cries. But his mother honors his loss by helping him bury Goldie. Julio recovers from his sadness. This is positive stress that has been mitigated by a supportive relationship. Supportive relationships, or protective factors, are adults in a child's life who provide consistent care and basic needs. This type of stress helps a child's system build up an ability to manage stressful situations later in life.

Tolerable stress might be something that occurs in the life of a child that is longer in duration. Examples of tolerable childhood stress include the temporary absence of a parent, a lengthy illness, or, as discussed previously, a pandemic, for children with few to no ACEs. Tolerable stress is tolerable because of the presence of supportive relationships or protective factors.

Toxic stress is chronic exposure to adverse experiences without the presence of supportive relationships. Prolonged toxic levels of stress in childhood is one of the factors contributing to the poor adult health outcomes discussed previously.

When the ANS is activated in response to a stressful situation, it creates a fight-flight-freeze response—an autonomic response originally coined by Walter Cannon in 1929 (Cannon, 1994) that happens without planning (Siegel, 2012). The amygdala and the hippocampus exist in the subconscious brain. When violence or a natural disaster threatens the safety of a person, their ANS triggers, the stress-response system activates and the person,

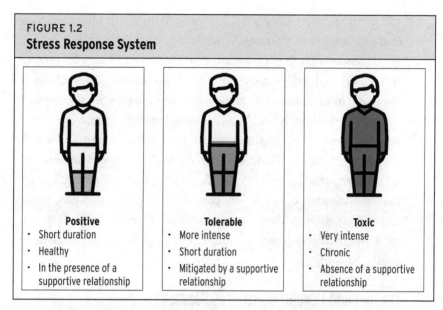

FIGURE 1.2
Stress Response System

Positive	Tolerable	Toxic
• Short duration	• More intense	• Very intense
• Healthy	• Short duration	• Chronic
• In the presence of a supportive relationship	• Mitigated by a supportive relationship	• Absence of a supportive relationship

Source: Adapted with permission from "What are ACEs," 2021, at www.originstraining.org/our-approach/#aces.

responds to the threat by holding still, running away from the per-ceived threat, or defending themselves against the threat (Porges & Carter, 2017).

We share this survival response with other mammals. Horses are largely flight animals. In the case of a barn fire, horses will do what-ever it takes to escape the barn. Imagine you come upon a barn on fire. You might open the door to the barn so that the horses could escape. You would also probably get out of the way. A horse in flight will run over even their most beloved human—not because it is a bad horse, but because the survival instinct takes over and logic and reason are absent until safety is achieved. A dog being chased by a hungry bear will likely run away; it might even run out into traffic to escape the threat posed by the bear. This same dog, when he runs out of space and is backed into a corner by the bear, will turn and fight. The freeze response is best illustrated by a deer caught in the head-lights of an oncoming car, overwhelmed by the sights, the sounds, and the smells of the highway. The flood of toxic stress hormones can cause the system to shut down. Movement becomes impossible.

Students with DT, in response to perceived threats to physical and emotional safety, may have an exaggerated fight-flight-freeze response. In the classroom, they might demonstrate a fight response by cursing, stealing, lying, throwing things, or becoming aggressive to peers or adults. They might demonstrate a flight response by leaving the room or silently refusing to participate. They might demonstrate a freeze response by pulling their hood up, putting their head down, staring into space, or simply not coming to school at all. These behaviors are not choices. These are responses to the brain's signals for survival—signals that death is imminent and survival must be achieved at all costs.

Trauma and Psychological Development

In addition to the neurobiological effects, trauma has a significant effect on psychological development. Attachment is a psychological, evolutionary, and ethological concept regarding relationships between humans (Bowlby, 1982). Young children need to develop a relationship with at least one primary caregiver for normal social and emotional development (Bowlby et al., 1989). Attachment occurs while we are picking up our babies, holding them, telling them they will be okay, and looking at them. Attachment develops when we stare, forever fascinated, at our babies' faces. Attachment happens when we feed our children dinner every night. Children with trauma may have intermittent experience with parental gazing. They may begin forming healthy attachment that is interrupted by a parent who is no longer physically or emotionally available. This results in delayed development of the internal working model (IWM; Verschueren et al., 1996). The IWM is a representation of self that we each carry around with us. It develops and strengthens when a child receives consistent care and trusting relationships. A functioning IWM is necessary for trust to develop. Establishing relationships is necessary for survival. Children

with an impaired or absent IWM have difficulty establishing relationships and regulating behavior. They have learned that trust, which is
required for the development of healthy relationships, is dangerous.
They often have intense feelings of hopelessness. They experience
extreme shame, and they have little sense of self (Schore, 2009). This
interferes with their ability to develop self-regulation, self-determina-
tion, and self-efficacy. *Self, self, self.* You need a self to develop any of
these capacities. Children without a healthy IWM have a skewed or
absent sense of self. They cannot engage in self-talk.

There are four basic styles of attachment (see Figure 1.3). **Secure
attachment** develops when a child's basic needs are consistently met
and when they receive sufficient caregiver gazing during infancy and
early childhood. Children with secure attachment are able to establish relationships with their classmates and their teachers. They are
able to ask for help. They believe that someone will help them. They
believe they are worthy of being helped. They are curious about their
environment.

The other three types of attachment are more fragile: **preoccupied, fearful,** or **dismissive.** Anxious ambivalent children can be
clingy. They may be overdependent on attention from adults, teachers, and peers. They can demonstrate jealousy. They tend to want all
the teacher's attention. The 3rd grade student who still seems to need
to sit on the teacher's lap might be demonstrating this kind of attachment. They may demonstrate attention-seeking behaviors to remain
the center of the class's attention. These children seem to "wear out"
their friends.

Children with avoidant fearful attachment seem to love you and
then hate you. They can be "come-but-go" in their relationship styles.
They may develop a close relationship with a teacher and then, for
seemingly no reason, sabotage that relationship. These children might
be called heartbreakers. This relationship style can also be seen in their
connections with their peers. They may vacillate between having a lot
of friends and having no friends at all—everybody likes me, nobody

likes me. These students may sabotage their relationship with you. They might work closely with you to complete a long-term project, and then on the date that the project is due, fail to turn it in for credit.

Avoidant dismissive children tend to avoid relationships with everyone. They often strive to be invisible in schools. They might not appreciate or anticipate relationships with adults or peers. This style of fragile attachment is not as common as the other two.

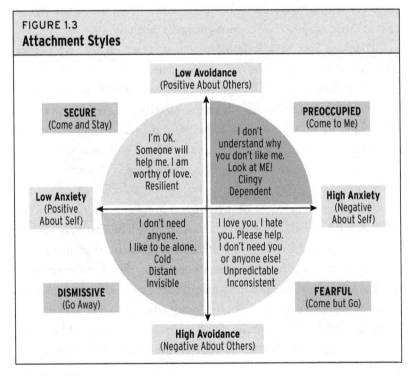

FIGURE 1.3
Attachment Styles

© 2022 Melissa Sadin

attachment

Attachment is all about relationships. Relationships can wound, but they can also heal. This is where we see how important it is for educators to understand the effects of trauma on our students. Relationships are the single most effective response to early childhood trauma. I'll have more about this in later chapters.

Another Paradigm Shift

Time for another paradigm shift. The child development courses included in most preservice teaching programs are largely based on a blend of cognitive behavior theory and social learning theory. Cognitive behavior theory posits that a person's thoughts about a situation or event influence their emotional reactions and behavior. Social learning theory holds that children learn by observing the adults around them (Bandura et al., 1996). Thus, if children observe respectful and compassionate behavior from their teachers, they should demonstrate those behaviors. As we know, children do not always mirror the behavior of their teachers. When a child is amygdala driven, they are technically *not* thinking when they are acting in an inappropriate way. The traumatology framework and attachment theory have shown that a child's behavior is more a result of their neurological development and early care than observation of others. Observation is still an important part of a child's development, but there is more to it.

We are all the product of our lived experiences, adverse and positive. The ACEs study and ongoing research show us that what happens to us as children has a significant influence on our neurobiological development and adult health outcomes (Anda et al., 2010; van der Kolk, 2005). But before we seek to understand our students, we must first dig around in our own invisible backpacks. It is important to know your ACE score and your resilience score. Understand the effects your cultural and religious upbringing has on the way you view the world—and on the way you see your students. You are more likely to recognize what has happened to your students if you first recognize what has happened to you. You are also more likely to embrace the paradigm shift necessary to provide trauma-informed instruction and create a resilient classroom and school community if you start with yourself.

Teachers should start w/ themselves

2

The Effects of Trauma on Learning and Behavior

Without a doubt, early childhood trauma affects learning and behavior. Sometimes behavior can affect learning, and sometimes learning affects behavior. In particular, the hippocampus—which you'll recall from Chapter 1 helps us regulate emotions—plays a role in the development of working, short-term, and long-term memory; processing speed; language development; executive functions; and emotional regulation—all of which are crucial to learning and behavior development.

Early Childhood Trauma and Learning

How trauma affects the limbic system ultimately has a profound influence on learning. The hippocampus is involved in many of our executive functions, including language development, memory, and processing speed.

Executive Functions

Executive functions are a set of cognitive capacities that act in a coordinated way. These directive abilities are responsible for a person's capacity to engage in purposeful, organized, strategic, self-regulated, and goal-directed processing of perceptions, emotions, thoughts, and actions (Strosnider & Sharpe, 2019). It is important to note that executive functions are not responsible for what we think and feel; rather, they help us use our perceptions, thoughts, and feelings in a constructive way. Many of our executive functions engage our hippocampus. If trauma has interrupted the development of the hippocampus, then often some or all executive functions will be absent or delayed. What might it look like if a student is struggling with one of the capacities of executive functions?

- **Attention.** Directing the attentional processes, including filtering interference, attention to task, and the inhibition of impulsive calling out. Children with delays in this area of executive function might call out or say inappropriate things. They might raise their hand, wait to be called on, and then state something that has nothing to do with the lesson. Children who struggle with attentional processes may not be able to filter out distractions, which can include sounds, smells, clothing, or a poorly adjusted desk or chair.
- **Judgment and Task Organization.** Initiating judgment about the amount of time or effort that a task requires. Students with challenges in this area often feel defeated by an assignment before they even get started. They might lack time management. They might resist starting assignments with more than a few questions. Or they may give up after completing a few pieces of the activity.
- **Processing Speed.** Regulating the speed of information processing. This can be auditory or visual information. Students who struggle with visual processing speed often have difficulties learning to read. Students with auditory processing speed issues may struggle with lecture format. They will have problems following multistep directions. They may look like they are not paying attention.
- **Working Memory.** Directing the ability to hold and manipulate information. Students who struggle with working memory

often ask you to repeat directions. They can be looking right at you and as soon as you finish with the directions, they say, "What?" I call them the "Wait. What?" kids. Their challenges can stem from a combination of problems involving auditory processing, working memory, and receptive language (see the next section). These students will almost certainly struggle with mental math.

- **Long-Term Memory.** Directing the efficient placement of information. Students might be able to take in information and understand its meaning, but their long-term memory function doesn't know where to put it. Students who struggle with long-term memory might be engaged in a lesson on Monday, participating in the discussion and completing the assignment, then show up on Tuesday and have no recollection of what happened the day before. These students may also struggle with homework completion. They tell their parents and caregivers that they don't remember what happened in class or that the teacher did not tell them how to complete the homework activity.

- **Writing.** Directing the collaboration of multiple abilities to produce written responses that represent the level of their understanding. Students who struggle in this area might provide simple one- or two-sentence written responses, even though they have in-depth understanding of the information. They might avoid writing or struggle to get started on an essay. These students can often provide an organized response orally but resist writing it down.

Language Development

Language is both part of the executive functions and a separate area of development. The production of sensible language in response to a prompt is part of the executive functions. Children who struggle in this area may have difficulty providing answers that are germane to the topic being learned or discussed.

When we look at language as a separate area of development, however, we are talking about expressive and receptive language development. Be aware that language development is a highly complex concept. Expressive and receptive language development cannot be considered completely separate from the executive functions that help operate our language reception, expression, and retention. There is also complex overlap between language development and memory. Childhood trauma can delay or prevent the development of some or all the language processes (Merritt & Klein, 2015).

Receptive language is the process through which we take in written and oral language. Expressive language is the process through which we communicate our thoughts and feelings using writing or the spoken word. In between receiving and expressing information is the storing of that information in a way that allows us to find it and use it. (That is the part that crosses over into executive function and memory.) Imagine our brains as gigantic warehouses filled with thousands of file cabinets. When we learn a word, that word gets stored in a file cabinet based on what it is, what it does, and what it means. A word can get stored in one drawer and have a piece of yarn connecting it to another drawer indicating cross-meaning and connection to other concepts. As we grow, the warehouse fills with file cabinets and massive amounts of yarn crisscrossing the space and connecting drawers to one another.

Consider 5-year-old Juanita. Juanita has age-appropriate expressive and receptive language development. She also has typically developed working and long-term memory. When Juanita learns about yellow, for example, she learns that it is a color. The word "yellow" gets stored in a drawer with other colors. But it also has yarn connecting it to raincoats that can be yellow and bananas that are often yellow. Thus Juanita is able to learn the word "yellow," make meaning of the word, and store it away for future use.

Expressive language is engaged when Juanita wants to express her understanding of the word "yellow" by identifying it in a picture and using it correctly in her spoken language. This is the part of the process that involves memory—knowing where to find the word "yellow" based on context. With typically developing language skills, Juanita will be able to respond appropriately to a question like, "Can you point to the yellow shape on this page?" She will also be able to respond to a question like, "Can you tell me the color of ripe bananas?"

Now consider 6-year-old Teddy. Teddy has receptive and expressive language delays. He also struggles with working memory. When Teddy learns about yellow, he may put the word in the correct color drawer, but struggle with the yarn that connects it to other items such as raincoats and bananas. So, Teddy might be able to identify the color yellow in a shape, but when asked the color of ripe bananas, he may not know. Teddy may also need more time to find the word and its meaning and give it back. For instance, if you ask Teddy, "What is the color of the sun?" he may look away, or he may look right at you for an extended pause, and then be able to give you the answer "yellow." Teddy may recognize yellow in the circle you show him one day, but not recognize it on a shirt the next.

Educators should be careful to explore both receptive and expressive language retention and development. Too often, when Teddy does not provide the correct answer, his teacher may assume he wasn't paying attention. It's possible, however, that Teddy was paying attention the previous day when the class learned about the color yellow, but his brain cannot find where it stored the meaning of the word. Or it's possible he stored it properly but failed to connect it to other similar contexts.

Educators working with dual-language or English language learners should keep in mind that trauma can impede the development of both the native and second language. More than 50 percent of our nation's recent immigrants and refugees are school-age children.

Trauma from leaving native country

Children who have recently left or escaped their native countries may endure multiple ACEs during their journey. In addition, they may have experienced community and household ACEs prior to their immigration to the United States (Kaplan et al., 2016).

It is essential that children continue to speak, read, and write in their native language while learning their second language, for preservation of culture as well as development of language. If the first-language acquisition is affected by trauma, it is common for the second language to develop more slowly. Immersion programs where students are taught in their native language while learning the same concepts in English have shown positive results (Medley, 2012). Although the complex needs of multilingual students are beyond the scope of this book, many resources are available that you can consult alongside this book to help you prepare trauma-informed, culturally affirming IEPs that take multilingual learners' needs into consideration. (See, for example, The National Association for the Education of Young Children at www.naeyc.org and *Teaching Dual Language Learners: What Early Childhood Educators Need to Know* by Lisa López and Mariela Páez.)

Cognition

Cognition refers to the process of acquiring knowledge, organizing the information, and applying the knowledge. Cognition is more than intelligence quotient (IQ), but IQ is a part of cognition. Studies have shown that childhood trauma may affect cognition as well as overall IQ scores (Enlow et al., 2012). The causes for cognitive delay can include parental IQ, parental attachment, and exposure to personal or environmental violence after birth. Parental socioeconomic status (SES) and delayed language development are also connected.

Children who live with shelter insecurity and food insecurity may be living with parents or caregivers who are in survival mode, for example. They may not have lengthy dinner conversations. They may not have the capacity or time for a bedtime story every night.

Shelter/food insecurity

Socioeconomic

They may use simple and concrete vocabulary. They may have limited education, which can account for job insecurity, leading to food and shelter insecurity, and so on. Children with delayed or limited cognition may be from three to five years behind their peers of the same age across all areas of executive function and language development. Delayed cognitive ability will affect language development, writing, reading, math aptitude, and memory.

How many of the students who come to mind as you read through this book struggle with all, most, or some of the above capacities? Executive functions are the tools that students use to apply what they see, hear, understand, and learn in class. When these tools have been delayed in their development, learning in a traditional way becomes challenging. Language is the key to everything. It is the way students take in information, store it, and give it back. Childhood trauma can affect any part of the development of executive functions and language.

Many of the instructional strategies that have been shown to be effective for children with trauma are strategies that have already been identified as excellent instruction for all students. Implementing trauma-informed teaching strategies that are applied in general education and special education settings alike will improve the academic outcomes for all students. I will explore these strategies in the next chapter.

Early Childhood Trauma and Behavior

A child's behavior is influenced by their attachment style and the development of their ANS: nature and nurture. As we discussed in Chapter 1, children who have experienced trauma are largely amygdala driven. As a result of their exposure to trauma, their amygdala, their survival brain, remains on high alert, with the cortisol, adrenaline, and other stress response hormones released in high quantities. This flood of toxic stress hormones delays the development of other parts of the limbic system, specifically the hippocampus, which is responsible for the development of emotional regulation, and the prefrontal cortex, which is involved in making choices (Hanson et al., 2014).

Let's discuss this in terms of behavior in school. Traumatized children, driven by their overactive amygdala, can be hyperaroused; they tend to view their world as dangerous and unpredictable and thus are prepared to react at a moment's notice, sometimes in inappropriate and possibly unsafe ways (as illustrated with the horse example in Chapter 1). They can also be hypervigilant and on the lookout for perceived threats to their safety. Because hyperarousal and hypervigilance lead to delayed development of the hippocampus, which helps them to regulate in times of stress, these traumatized children are unable to distinguish between a real threat to safety (a building on fire) and an imagined one (a poor grade on a test).

Executive Functions

Executive functions play a role in behavior as well as learning. Early childhood trauma can delay or impair the capacities outlined here because of their interconnectedness with the limbic system. The purpose of this discussion is to help educators (1) resist the temptation to assume the student has a lack of care, lack of remorse, lack of focus, and so on; and (2) understand that explicit instruction of executive function capacities can help to grow and develop the hippocampus. Children with trauma can learn to regulate their emotions and behavior through the development of these executive functions and through relationships. They may, however, need explicit instruction. They may not be learning it simply by observing the interactions of others.

- **Social Development.** Initiating the engagement of appropriate social behavior. Thinking back to our discussion of social learning theory, even if a child with developmental trauma (DT) learns by observing the behavior of others, they may not to be able to access that behavior in times of stress. Their amygdala

trauma
excess cortisol

may fire and produce copious amounts of cortisol and block the connection to this learned behavior. (Once I learned this, I gave up the comment, "You should know better" almost completely.)

- **Perspective.** Accessing the ability to take the perspective of someone else. So much of my training as a teacher involved asking children, "How would you feel if someone did that to you?" When children respond that they don't know, teachers sometimes become frustrated. They assume that children over the age of 7 or 8 should be aware of the feelings of others, and that may be the case when their brains are developing neurotypically. Be careful not to assume that students don't care or lack remorse. Kids who have experienced trauma often can't imagine how they would feel until their hippocampus develops more. They struggle to take the perspective of someone else without explicit instruction. Telling students how someone else might feel may help develop this ability over time.

Kids w/ trauma can't imagine how others feel

- **Emotional Regulation.** Signaling the regulation of emotional control. Children with DT often have delayed hippocampal development. Consider Tawana. Tawana is a typically developing child with no evidence of trauma exposure. At 3 to 4 years old, she may believe monsters live under her bed and need a parent or caregiver to come and check to reassure her that she is safe and that there are no monsters. As Tawana's brain develops, the hippocampus grows and starts to mimic the care provided by her parents. At 5 years old, Tawana might be scared one night as she lies in bed and listens to a storm outside her window. Without cognitive intention or choice, Tawana's brain sends her messages that she is okay. Tawana has developed the ability to override her initial feelings of fear. Note that at 5 years old, Tawana is not necessarily making a choice. The regulation of her emotions is happening automatically. At 9 years old, after watching a scary movie that her parents told her she was too young to watch, Tawana might lie in bed and talk to herself. She might list the reasons she knows she is safe and that monsters are not in her closet with chain saws. Her ability to regulate is becoming a choice.

Now consider Jenna. Jenna is living with parents who are violent with each other. She is often hungry and ignored by her parents. Jenna's hippocampus is likely not developing appropriately. Instead, her amygdala remains in charge because she has not had consistent care or felt safety. At 3 to 4 years old, she may believe monsters live under her bed, but when she calls, no one comes to reassure her. Her fears escalate, increasing the production of toxic stress hormones. Her amygdala grows and her hippocampus does not. At 5 years old, Jenna is disproportionately afraid of the storm outside her bedroom window. She lies awake most of the night. By 9 years old, Jenna does not really know what it means to feel safe. She sees threats and dangers where Tawana does not. She cannot choose to regulate her emotions. (This is why you should not tell kids to "calm down.")

[handwritten margin note: Cannot regulate emotions hippocampus does not develop]

- **Prediction.** Initiating the capacity to use hindsight as a learning tool or to use foresight to avoid problems. Children with DT often do not learn from their mistakes. A child with DT who gets in trouble for pushing in line may not be able to use that as a lesson to not push outside on the playground. The brain has not developed the capacity. It is often not a choice or a complete disregard of your caring conversation about what might happen if the child pushes again. (This is why you should stop asking, "How many times have I told you. . . ?" or "When are you going to learn that . . . ?")

[handwritten margin note: Cannot learn from mistake or apply to other areas]

Classroom Management and Behavior Response

Many teachers learn about classroom management and behavior response implicitly and explicitly. Sadly, preservice teaching programs often have little direct or explicit instruction regarding classroom management. Most of what teachers learn about behavior response comes from implicitly adopting the processes, practices, and language already used in their schools. Basically, they figure out that they should reward good behavior and ignore or punish bad behavior. The reward and the punishment are often determined by the whole school program. Some schools have stores where children can redeem their tickets or points earned for good behavior, and they encourage children to take responsibility for their actions by explaining what they did. The teachers expect children to learn from their mistakes by exploring the reasons for their behavior and agreeing on an appropriate consequence. This can be an effective strategy for children who have age-appropriate reasoning skills and a sense of self derived from consistent care and attachment, but it's problematic for children who have experienced trauma.

In addition to the cognitive approach, teachers and schools might employ the traditional method of reward and punishment—the behavioral theory in action. In fact, it seems that the more severe the behavior, the more swiftly an administrator or teacher moves from cognitive strategies to behavioral strategies. The problem with strict reward and punishment is that while it might have been an effective way to move mice through mazes, it does not translate cleanly to animals with higher-order brain functions. Punishing children may stop the unwanted behavior at a particular point in time, but it does not teach appropriate behavior. Eventually, you create a child who might hit or engage in other unproductive behaviors to solve problems. Rewards might encourage the desired behavior initially, but unless you move from the sticker chart to skills in self-regulation, the improvement will be short-lived.

Any type of punishing, yelling, or exclusion (detention or time out) can be a trigger for a child with DT. That child is already often on high alert for threats to their safety. When a student is triggered into survival mode by a trauma reminder, the "learning brain" largely goes offline. In this state, a child is neurobiologically unable to learn. The child's behavior is a normal response to toxic stress; it is not "willful" or intentionally directed. Children with trauma exposure are not ready for cognitive behavior strategies.

The good news is that young brains are flexible. Reduce toxic stress levels and diminish threats to safety, and the development of neural pathways through the hippocampus to the prefrontal cortex resumes (Hanson et al., 2014). Before schools can be physically safe places, they need to be emotionally safe places. When teachers and administrators understand the effects of trauma on children, and why those children are acting out, they can develop policies and procedures that consider the neurological state of their most frequent offenders and prepare an appropriate response. It is time for a paradigm shift.

Consider Iggy. Iggy came to kindergarten with a wonderful giggle and very little of anything else. As time went by, his teacher learned that he was living with his grandmother. His father was incarcerated, and his mother was gone. Iggy spent the first three years of his life living in poverty with a drug-addicted mother who would host large, loud parties until all hours of the night. He saw a lot of violence, and it is believed that he was physically abused as well. At the age of 4, he was taken from his mother by child protective services. His grandmother filed for full custody. His grandmother loved him; he came to school clean and wearing appropriate clothing. In September, Iggy ran out of the classroom multiple times a week. He would run around the halls. He rarely left the building but would pull things off the walls on his way by. Usually, when it was time for him to sit and engage in an assignment, he would laugh as he ran circles around the classroom. He took things that did not belong to him and helped himself to learning supplies without asking. Occasionally, he would grab what he wanted away from classmates. He was largely uncontrollable in the lunchroom. At recess, he would run constantly but never seemed to engage with his peers or play organized games.

A traditional view of this behavior would be that Iggy was atten-tion seeking and needed to be taught manners. A behavior plan might be put in place. Iggy would get stickers for completing a task or staying in the classroom. He might even receive a consequence for running around the school or classroom. But what typically occurs in response to a plan like this for children with DT is that behaviors escalate and become more disruptive and unsafe. Iggy might spend a great deal of time with the school counselor or the building administrator. Over time, his behaviors would most certainly result in detention and sus-pension. We will talk more about the effects of traditional behavior plans on children with trauma in Chapter 5.

A trauma-informed view of this scenario considers what had happened to Iggy, not what was wrong with Iggy. Iggy had fragile attachment from his early years with his birth mother. A thorough investigation of his background could yield as many as eight ACEs. He was unable to trust and became dysregulated by the amount of sensory information present in a typical kindergarten class. He was hypervigilant and hyperaroused. He responded by demonstrating dysregulated behavior.

Now consider what we have learned about the role of executive function and behavior. Iggy did not possess the capacity to understand how his running around the classroom might be affecting others. If his hippocampus had developed the ability to regulate, he could not access it. He could not filter the noises and conversation going on throughout the day in his classroom. He might have a language delay and most certainly was not processing anything his teacher was saying to him while he was running around the classroom. Basically, Iggy was giving the best that he had.

Threatening, punishing, restraining, and isolating do not yield positive results for kids with trauma because they are operating from a different place developmentally than students without trauma. They are getting messages from their brains that they are not safe. Most of what they do, no matter how misguided, is actually an attempt to be safe. Iggy was running from his teacher for a number of reasons. None of those reasons was choice. He was not doing it just to irritate his teacher, although one can certainly understand why it might look like he was. The next chapter explores fully what we might do for students like Iggy, but first we need to explore more reasons for a paradigm shift in the way we respond to behavior in schools.

Disproportionality Revisited

In traditional public school settings, teachers respond to behavior problems in their classrooms with reactive strategies such as time out, removal from class, isolation, and restraint. These are strategies that we do *to* children, not *with* them. Such strategies may increase acting out or withdrawal behaviors for children with DT. Responding authoritatively to a child who is demonstrating amygdala-driven behavior may simply increase the demonstration of those behaviors and, thus, make the behavior worse, not better. Teachers who employ reactive strategies often claim that they are only following school policy, or they are acting on some form of internal belief that "someone needs to teach these kids right from wrong."

Whole school approaches to discipline have been largely exclusionary and reactive for the past 20 years. Exclusionary school climates are those in which teachers or administrators remove students from class or school for a determined period for minor infractions as well as for major ones without consideration of each individual child's history. This concept of exclusion, commonly referred to as "zero-tolerance," came in response to the school shootings at Columbine High School in 1999. Many school districts revitalized their commitment to exclusionary practices after the Elementary and Secondary Education Act (ESEA) was reauthorized in 2002 and became known as the No Child Left Behind Act (NCLB). NCLB required more accountability from school districts by increasing the rigor of standardized tests and calling for higher student achievement on those tests. This may have encouraged teachers and administrators to redouble their efforts at removing children from the learning environment so that they would not distract other students from learning.

However, this effort to make schools safe may have come at the expense of the students with DT, students of color, and students receiving special education. Almost half of all children suspended in the United States are Black (Ryan & Goodram, 2013). Children receiving special education services are more likely to be suspended (Skiba et al., 2014), as are children living in poverty (Ryan & Goodman, 2013). Thus, children with DT may be oversuspended in exclusionary schools because of overrepresentation in special education and low SES groups, thereby preventing them from attending the very place that could potentially mitigate the effects of their trauma.

Intergenerational trauma is another type of trauma that is overrepresented in the suspension and exclusion data (Brendtro et al., 2014). Intergenerational trauma is trauma that is experienced by a group or generation of people that is handed down to the children through nature and nurture. Native American children, Black children, and many children living in intergenerational poverty or abuse may experience intergenerational trauma. Children with intergenerational trauma often feel hopeless. They may experience the weight of the grief of previous generations without the acknowledgement of the problem or language to express it (Brendtro et al., 2014). They may have expressed the feeling that there is something wrong with them, that they are to blame for the state of their family or people, yet they are unable to grieve (Barron & Abdallah, 2015). Native Americans have been shown to be overrepresented in high school discipline data and in juvenile justice records (Brendtro et al., 2014).

So we are back to that need for a paradigm shift. If we keep doing what we have always done, we will keep getting what we have always gotten—education that is culturally incompetent and harmful to children. We need schoolwide and individual strategies to be more proactive than reactive. We need programs and strategies for *working with* children, not *doing things to* children. We'll explore specific strategies and programs in Chapter 3.

3

Trauma-Informed Instruction and the CARES Framework

Developmental trauma (DT) is a not a mental *illness,* but a mental *injury* that educators can help to heal with trauma-informed instructional strategies and behavior response strategies that address the effects of trauma. Because IEPs are only as good as the teachers who are responsible for carrying them out, it is crucial for *all* teachers, general and special education, to understand the effects of trauma on learning and behavior and how that understanding should inform their instruction.

Resilience is the cure for the effects of trauma on neurobiological development. Resilience can be defined as the ability to adapt to a changing environment and overcome obstacles (Zolkoski & Bullock, 2012). The ability to adapt and overcome is something we want for all our children. Trauma-informed teaching and behavior response builds resilience. In a resilience-based classroom, teachers focus on relationships, instruction explicitly targets the development of executive functions, and activities are designed to grow the hippocampus and thus increase regulation strategies for all students. In fact, many of the instructional strategies that have been shown to build resilience for children with trauma are strategies that have already

How Trauma Inf. Works

been identified as excellent instruction for all students. Thus, trauma-informed teaching is excellent teaching for all.

Children develop resilience when they feel safe, find connection and attachment in school, learn to and have the opportunity to get regulated, and learn through explicit instruction of executive function skills. Consider the CARES framework outlined in Figure 3.1. In all my years as a teacher and administrator, I have never met a teacher, paraprofessional, staff member, or administrator who did not *care*. We just need to take that care and apply it to what we now know about the neurobiology of trauma.

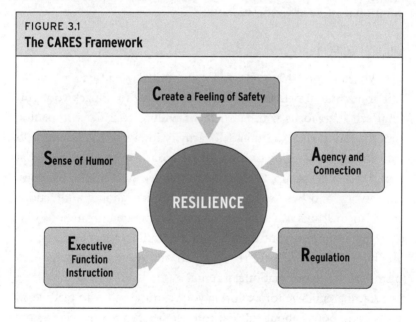

FIGURE 3.1
The CARES Framework

Create a Feeling of Safety

Because many children with trauma are amygdala driven, they perceive the world to be a dangerous place. This overarching condition might cause them to misunderstand the meaning of a classmate's actions. They may appear distracted or extremely withdrawn. When we create the feeling of safety—specifically emotional safety—we see a decrease in the aforementioned protective behaviors. Of course, the physical safety of everyone in the school is of primary importance. All of us must feel safe from physical harm to perform our roles in the school. Doors should be locked. Everyone should know what to do in case of fire or an intruder. Attention to emotional safety comes after physical safety has been assured. You can create a feeling of safety in your space or classroom in a number of ways, but the most important piece of felt safety in the classroom is *you*. Who you are, what has happened to you, and what you say are all building blocks for creating emotional safety in your classroom.

Cultural Competence

Who are you? Where do you come from? What are your political and spiritual beliefs? The best way I know to unpack your cultural self is to focus within. To focus within, consider completing the "Exploring Your Cultural Self" activity in Figure 3.2. You can do this activity on your own, in small groups, or in small groups that report to a larger group. Look for unconscious bias—that is, attitudes, stereotypes, and beliefs that affect your understanding and actions in an unconscious way. The best way to eliminate unconscious bias is to dig around in your cultural self and build your awareness. Do you have white privilege? Are you a part of a group that has endured historical or intergenerational trauma?

Another strategy for exploring your cultural self is to read. Read or listen to books about cultural competence, white privilege, equity in schools, gender identity, sexual orientation, and so on. Read historical fiction and nonfiction about the ethnic groups that make up your student body. Did you grow up with shelter or food insecurity? Chances are that many of the students who attend your school are living with those insecurities. If you did not experience them, read about them so that you have a greater understanding of your students.

FIGURE 3.2
Exploring Your Cultural Self

Write your name in the middle of the circle. In the surrounding circles, write words you would use to describe your cultural self (e.g., Latina, female, Jewish, dyslexic). You can add as many circles as necessary to list your relevant identifiers.

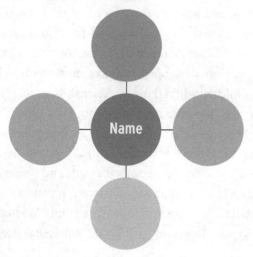

In a small group,

1. Share one of the descriptors you are proud of and a time when the descriptor was appreciated by others.
2. Share one of the descriptors that you are not proud of and a time when the descriptor caused you discomfort.

Remember: You are more than the labels society uses to describe you.

Think about your students.

- Do any of them fit into any of your descriptors?
- How many other descriptors are represented in your class?
- What can you do to help your students understand your cultural self?
- What can you do to learn about your students' cultural selves?

Join a book study. That gives you the added benefit of processing your understanding with others. Host a book study in your school.

A third strategy is to talk to people. After you read a few books, you will likely be more comfortable discussing race, religion, and culture with others in a sensitive and competent way. Many books are available to help you navigate these issues in your classroom. All students need to feel that they are accepted for who they are. Children are attuned to our biases. Think back to your own years in school. You knew which teachers were open and accepting and which ones were judging you. Children with DT are hypersensitive to real and imagined bias. We have to go the extra mile when communicating that our classrooms are safe places where students are all free to be who they are. Do not assume that your students know it. Say it. Repeatedly. Communicate it visually in your classroom with signs and posters. Be vigilant about the way you allow students to interact in your classroom. From prekindergarten to 12th grade, frequently stating, "We treat each other with respect in this classroom" will hold you in good stead.

Language and Word Choice

Another way to create a feeling of safety in your classroom is with language. Your words matter! As I suggested in the previous chapter, you may want to spend a few days really listening to what you are saying to your students. Much of what you say was probably said to you as a child. We can change those habits.

Have you ever said to a child: *"What is wrong with you?"* This is a great way to let kids know you think there is something wrong with them. What about *"How many times have I told you . . . ?"* Kids hear, *"Obviously you are too stupid to learn."* Of course, you would never call a student stupid, but you must think about how your students hear what you say. Have you ever had a conversation like this:

Teacher: How many times have I told you to take notes?
Student: I don't know . . . 50?
Teacher: Don't be snarky!

Many children with trauma are quite literal. I cannot count the number of times that a student who was sent to my office after an exchange like the previous one told me that they believed the teacher thinks they are stupid. Children without trauma can be literal, too, but are better prepared to unpack what the teacher really means to say. But if you say what you mean, and mean what you say, you will make great strides toward creating that feeling of safety in your classroom. (A note about sarcasm: Use it with great care and on an individual basis. To my middle school friends: I know that sarcasm can be the language of middle school students. I just ask you to tread carefully. Check for understanding once in a while.)

Consider Shane. When Shane was in middle school, he struggled with the increased number of teachers as he transitioned from elementary school. Shane is a great example of a student with DT who needs relationships and trust to be able to learn. He found relationships and trust with many of his amazing teachers in middle school, but not all his teachers understood or accepted his need for felt safety and trust. One of his teachers, Mrs. Smith, just seemed to connect with Shane. Even better, he had her for two years as she changed her teaching assignment. He thrived in her class even though her content area was not one he had prospered in previously. After their first six months or so together, Mrs. Smith learned that Shane had a terrific sense of humor. She used that to engage him and help him regulate.

Shane did not have a strong relationship with Mr. Lopez in another class. One day Mr. Lopez, in response to his frustration that Shane was constantly interrupting his lesson, said, "Did I stutter?" in response to Shane asking for clarification regarding instructions for the class activity. It is likely that Shane was busy telling jokes and talking to classmates when the directions were given. Shane replied, "I don't know. I haven't noticed." Mr. Lopez sent Shane to the building administrator for being disrespectful. Shane became dysregulated. He began yelling and cursing. Luckily, Mrs. Smith came into the office and, overhearing Shane, inserted herself into the situation.

Shane calmed down and was able to resume his day. When Mrs. Smith recounted the events to me later, she explained that Shane was embarrassed that he didn't realize that Mr. Lopez was using sarcasm. Shane continued to struggle in that class but managed to pass for the year. He still struggles with subtle forms of sarcasm. I'm not sure it was Shane who was disrespectful.

Another phrase to beware of is *"Why did you do that?"* In fact, get out of the *"why"* game completely. Neurotypical children under the age of 10 can rarely answer that question without prompting. Neurotypical children over the age of 10 might lie to avoid prosecution. They might deny knowing why because they are ashamed by what they have done. Children with hyperarousal and amygdala-driven actions often do not know why they did what they did. Asking them why only serves to increase their shame.

Children feel safe when they understand you and feel that you understand them. So, what *should* you say to your students? Anything that is from the heart or conveys that you care. Also, anything that avoids increasing the shame that many children with trauma feel. Remember our discussion about attachment in Chapter 1? Kids with fragile attachment may have a diminished sense of self-worth. They may walk through life looking through a lens of complete unworthiness. Here are some relationship-building statements that you might consider working into your repertoire instead:

- "It looks like you are struggling. How can I help?
- "What's in your way?"
- "I noticed . . . ."
- "Let's work together to . . . ."
- "Can you show me . . . ."
- "I need you to _____. How can I help you get there?"

Consistency

Finally, children feel safe when there is consistency in their environment—consistency in the daily routine of your classroom, in your treatment of your students, in the way you communicate and carry out your classroom rules and expectations, with schoolwide policies and procedures. Keep in mind that consistency is not everyone getting the same thing but everyone getting what they need, consistently.

Let's think about classroom rules and expectations. Do you have them posted on your wall? How many are there? Try to keep your rules limited to between three and five in number. No one can keep 10 rules in their minds at all times. Consider the following three rules:

1. Take care of self.
2. Take care of others.
3. Take care of stuff.

These three simple rules can apply to anything that might happen in any classroom in any grade. For those of you who use responsive classroom practices and develop your rules with your students, try capturing all your students' suggestions on a piece of chart paper. Then ask your students to help you place them into three categories. Chances are pretty good that all the suggested rules fit into one of those three simple rules. I also encourage teachers to consider a schoolwide discussion of classroom rules and expectations. Students feel safe when they move from classroom to classroom and the rules and expectations are the same (Brady et al., 2015).

These three expectations are as effective in music class, art class, and physical education as they are in a content-based classroom. Be sure to teach your students what the three expectations look like in your space. Do not assume that students in the cafeteria will know what it looks like to take care of stuff in the lunchroom. Show them. Practice. After a few weeks, practice again. In an environment where expectations are shared, explained, and practiced, children feel safe. They begin to believe that they can succeed.

Every teacher in every grade, teaching any content, should start every lesson or class period with the following three questions:

1. What did we learn yesterday?

2. What is the next thing we need to learn?

3. Why are we learning about this topic?

This serves to connect previous learning to the day's lesson. It helps students place the learning in the broader unit and possibly make real-world connections. Many children, with and without trauma exposure, do not make these connections on their own. However, you help them learn to make connections by asking these three questions every day. It is also beneficial to close each lesson with an exit ticket or closure activity. You can use a variation of the opening questions to close the lesson:

1. What did we learn today?

2. What will we learn tomorrow?

3. Why are we learning this information?

You can create many variations on this theme. For example, try "One Aha! and One Question." Use sticky notes and ask each student to write down one thing they learned (the "aha") and one question they have. Collect these and start the next lesson by reviewing some of the ahas and answering some of the questions. This basic lesson format, applied consistently, helps students feel safe. They can predict how the class will flow. In addition, this exercise can serve to strengthen some of the executive function capacities such as attention, memory, and task organization.

Agency and Connection

As we discussed in Chapter 1, many children with childhood trauma struggle with attachment. They have difficulty participating in give-and-take relationships, often because they have not had any good models. Their brains are sending them signals that they are not safe, which in turn makes it difficult to trust. I find this to be one of the great divides between neurotypical children and children affected by trauma. Neurotypical children often trust as a matter of course. They feel worthy of the care they get from others. They may still struggle with the dynamics of learning to have respectful and mutually satis-fying relationships, but it is easier to learn the subtleties of interper-sonal relationships when you can trust the people with whom you are having the relationship or who, like teachers and counselors, are helping you navigate the relationship waters.

One of the best ways to build attachment in our students is to focus on agency. **Student agency** refers to the level of autonomy and power that a student experiences in the learning environment (Wil-liams, 2017). Student agency is linked with student voice. Agency gives students the power to take responsibility for their learning. It has also been connected to self-regulation (Moses et al., 2020), which we will get to further on in this chapter. Remember in Chapter 1 when we dis-cussed that one of the effects of trauma on children is that they do not develop the ability to have control over their lives? Consider children who live with a caregiver or parent who has a substance abuse prob-lem. Most children have no power to help their parent get sober. They do not develop a sense of agency. Meanwhile, toddlers who develop the ability to disagree with their parents are also developing the abil-ity to decide what they want, which contributes to agency and in turn contributes to secure attachment.

We can build agency in our students in so many ways. Some may already be in place in your school or classroom: things like student government, allowing students to select their courses in middle and high school, selection of clubs, or surveys about school climate and teacher preference. For our students with trauma, however, we need to blend relationship with agency. In addition to all the great school-wide programs and practices just listed, we need to build agency in our classrooms. You may have heard of my two favorite strategies for this: differentiation and academic choice.

Differentiation refers to the practice of tailoring the lesson to meet the needs of each individual student (Tomlinson, 2017). We can differentiate in content, process, product, and environment. Most IEPs provide for modification of one or all these areas. Special and general education teachers who understand how to differentiate to build agency will be better equipped to provide the modifications called for in a trauma-informed IEP. More about that in the next chapter.

Let's break it down because it is really a blending of choice and differentiation that best contributes to the development of agency.

- **Differentiation of Content.** We all must teach the content as laid out in our curriculum. We can, however, modify how we teach that content to meet the needs of each of our learners. Students cannot choose to make changes to the curriculum in place for a class, but they might be able to choose the book they read that goes with the curriculum.
- **Differentiation of Process.** This refers to the instructional strategies that we use during the delivery of a lesson. Are they whole group, small group, or individual? What about the use of a minilesson format? Is there a video? Use of media? Will your instruction be lecture or discovery? Basically, how will you deliver the information?
- **Differentiation of Product.** What will the student do? How will they show you what they learned? How will they practice or interact with the content?
- **Differentiation of Environment.** Where will the instruction take place? In a small group or large? In the general education or special education classroom? In a public or therapeutic school? This one is not always at the discretion of the classroom teacher. Sometimes the IEP will determine environment.
- **Academic Choice.** This is the opportunity for the students to choose how, when, where, and what they will be learning. I call this *weighted choice*. Ideally, we provide choice that is consistent with the cognitive level and developmental age of each of our students.

Consider Mr. Webb. Mr. Webb is a 6th grade literacy teacher working on figurative language with his class. His lesson plan is to review metaphor, simile, and idiom and have his students identify and expand on the use of figurative language in their current essay. The content of the lesson is figurative language. Mr. Webb plans to begin the lesson by asking the students to sit with a partner and fold a piece of paper so that it is divided into three columns. Mr. Webb will demonstrate, then ask the students to write each of the three terms that appear on the board at the top of each one of the columns on their paper. He will give students the opportunity to write down as many similes, metaphors, and idioms as they can think of in the appropriate column, then invite students to go through their essays and look for the use of figurative language in their writing. Finally, Mr. Webb will ask students to improve or enhance the figurative writing that is in their essay.

Shane (whom we met earlier in this chapter) is in Mr. Webb's literature class. You will recall that he has some trust issues. His relationship with Mr. Webb is fragile. Mr. Webb has made efforts to befriend Shane, but most of those efforts have been rebuffed. Shane has an average cognitive ability and some developmental language delay. (Thus, he doesn't always identify the meanings of words and can struggle to express himself because his language pathways are slow to locate the words he wants to use.) At the start of the lesson, Shane exhibits frustration. He doesn't want to work with a partner. He claims he does not know how to fold his paper. Mr. Webb checks on Shane's understanding of the figurative language terms to be sure that his frustration is not a symptom of not understanding the content. Having determined that Shane does indeed understand the terms, Mr. Webb knows he does not need to differentiate the content for Shane.

Mr. Webb does have an opportunity, however, to differentiate both *process* and *product* and provide for *choice*. If Shane feels threatened by working with others, he may be more engaged if he works by himself. There will be time to teach him to work with others when he feels more secure with his relationships. Maybe Shane feels more comfortable if he uses a computer and makes three columns with a table, thus offering a choice about process. The product can be differentiated by allowing Shane to choose to come up with examples of figurative language by himself or maybe identify examples of each type in a paragraph provided by Mr. Webb.

Shane chooses to work by himself on a laptop and come up with the words himself. Mr. Webb allows this even though he has some reservation that with Shane's language delay, he might struggle with that part. This demonstrates *weighted choice* because Mr. Webb is giving Shane a choice between two processes. After a few minutes of working, Shane begins to goof off and distract other students. When Mr. Webb checks in, Shane tells him that the assignment is stupid. Mr. Webb reminds Shane that he can always change his choice and try finding words in the provided paragraph. Shane grudgingly agrees. This combination works. Shane completes the assignment and seems genuinely pleased with himself. He remains appropriately engaged in the remainder of the lesson.

This lesson is an example of not only differentiation blended with choice, but also the slow development of a relationship between Mr. Webb and Shane. Mr. Webb's ability to give Shane choice allows Shane to begin to trust him. Shane is also developing some sense of agency. His choices helped to make him successful in the figurative language lesson. Obviously, it takes some time to develop agency in students. It's helpful when all the teachers in a school, both general and special education, are working to do so. That way, this type of differentiation blended with choice and relationship really begins to take root in students. It is essential for children with trauma, but just as beneficial for children who do not have any early childhood trauma.

Connection is another way to blend agency with relationship. Students feel connected in school when they agree with the following statements (Blum, 2005):

- I have at least one adult I feel comfortable talking to.
- I have at least one friend at school.
- I feel the discipline practices are fair and consistent.
- I like school.
- The teachers are supportive and caring.
- I believe in my own current and future academic progress.
- I participate in extracurricular activities.

Make sure that you check on every student. Avoid assuming that because you have a lot of students in extracurricular activities that all your students feel connected. Find the invisible students. Employ your data system to run the entire student body against attendance at all clubs, activities, and sports. Identify the names that are on the list of no activities. Meet with staff to identify who knows the students whose names are on the list. Find them. Check in with them. Ask about their connections to the staff and students. Now, not every student on that list is unconnected. I had a friend in high school who did not participate in any activities at school because she spent hours before and after school in a dance studio. So she was connected to something and someone; it just wasn't taking place at school. That's why it's important to talk to everyone.

In the elementary grades, make it a priority to interview each of your students before the winter break. Find out what they like to do after school. Ask them about their wishes and dreams. Ask them who they could talk to if they had a problem. Ask them to name a friend. Other strategies for connection include greeting students when they enter your classroom, talking to students in the hallway, and creating opportunities for them to join clubs or activities with students of all ages (these are more common in secondary schools than elementary schools).

Looking for student connections will help you find the "invisible students." It is not always the students who act out the most who are of greatest concern. The quiet students who come to school just enough and complete just enough classwork can stay on the fringes of the community. They do enough to stay off of our at-risk student lists, but those students may need us more.

Regulation

Regulation, for our purposes, refers to the ability to calm the stress response system, regulate breathing, and slow the heart rate. As we have discussed previously, the hippocampus plays a major role in the development of emotional regulation. As neurotypical children grow, they demonstrate greater emotional regulation. A 3-year-old might interrupt you while you are on the phone, despite your pleas for them to wait until you are finished with your call. An 8-year-old, on the other hand, might be unhappy, might sigh and roll their eyes and stomp away, but they can wait for you to finish your call. Children with DT often display the social-emotional skills of a child from three to five years younger than they are because that is the level of their limbic system development. These children can be impulsive and struggle to wait their turn, even if they are in the 9th grade.

Consider Nellie. At the age of 1, she is just learning to walk. She moves across the living room on trembling little legs and falls. She cries. An adult or caregiver nearby will likely pick her up and soothe Nellie. They will tell her she is okay and encourage her to try again. This pattern is repeated until Nellie is walking without assistance. Fast forward four years. Nellie is running with her friends down the sidewalk. She falls. Nellie is startled. But for a brief moment, you might observe her scanning herself for damage. She looks at her hands and knees. If she is not seriously injured, she may dust herself off, stand up, and continue after her friends. She recovers. She "gets over it." This is her hippocampus at work. It mimics the care she received for the previous five years of her life and, like a gate keeper for the amygdala, helps Nellie pause and assess before crying or seeking help.

Now consider Adam. Adam has five ACEs and does not always receive the consistent care that Nellie learned to count on in early childhood. When Adam learns to walk, he moves across the room on trembling little legs. He falls. He cries. But no one comes to soothe him. He cries for a while and then maybe sticks his thumb in his mouth in an effort to soothe himself. Eventually, Adam teaches himself to walk. Fast forward four years. Adam is running down the sidewalk with his friends. He falls. He might get right up and chase his friends without scanning because his hyperactive amygdala and developmentally delayed hippocampus have caused a condition called *interoception*. Some children with trauma histories block the receptors to hunger, pain, and other physical discomforts in an effort to ignore them and survive. Or Adam might not be able to overcome the shock of falling and remains on the ground until long after his friends have disappeared. He does not recover. He does not "get over it."

Students with delayed regulation skills often demonstrate externalizing (acting out) or internalizing (withdrawing) behaviors that far exceed what you think is appropriate for the situation. They often have bigger reactions than seems necessary. A student with an age-appropriate limbic system gets a few answers wrong on a quiz and might be disappointed or upset. They might ask the teacher to explain why their answers are wrong. They might go home and ask a parent. Or they might recover. They might "get over it." A child with delayed limbic system development who gets a few answers wrong might completely shut down. They'll sit with their head down and hoodie up for the rest of the period despite your offers to help; they might crumple up the paper and throw it out. They might even tell you that you stink and your class stinks. They might jump up and run out of the room. You are left standing there thinking, "I don't understand. They know I will work with them after school. They only got a few answers incorrect. They still passed the quiz." That is all logical thinking—if this student had access to the gate keeper and then to the thinking brain.

The good news is that you can teach children to regulate their emotions and, by doing so, actually increase hippocampal development.

Teaching students to regulate their emotions can improve their level of patience, their perseverance, and their ability to do something they really don't want to do. Basically, they can learn resilience. Regulation can and should be taught at every grade level and across all curriculum content areas. The adults in the building should model the use of regulation strategies. Students should be able to ask for time to regulate. Regulation opportunities should be proactive as well as reactive. Proactive use of regulation tools will serve to prevent off-task behavior, impulsivity, and time out of the classroom. Sometimes students find themselves feeling dysregulated in response to something that has happened and they access a tool in response to their dysregulation. Both applications are effective.

You can proactively implement regulation tools in individual classrooms or schoolwide. I strongly recommend that you start in your own classroom and work toward a whole school understanding. We want to avoid something like the following middle school scenario:

> Mrs. Sunshine, a 7th grade English teacher, learns about and understands the benefits of regulation in the classroom. She finds her students receptive. One of her students, Shreyes, becomes extraordinarily attached to his silicone sponge, in part because he has come to realize that he pays better attention when he has the sponge. One day he brings it to his math class, which follows English. His math teacher, Mrs. Crabtree, has *not* learned the benefits of regulation. She sees Shreyes with his sponge, and because she is concerned about it being a distraction, she tells Shreyes to "put his toy away." Shreyes panics that he is going to lose his tool, so he curses at Mrs. Crabtree and is sent to the office for being disrespectful.

Two crucial pieces to whole school implementation of regulation tools are that all the staff are taught the importance of regulation in academic performance and that students be taught about their limbic systems and why regulation is an important skill for them to learn. Several books are available to give you lessons and guides for teaching the limbic system from kindergarten through high school. *The MindUP Curriculum* series by the Hawn Foundation (2011) is an excellent resource, with levels for preK–2, grades 3–5, and grades 6–8. I have used the middle school level book with high school students without too much need for modification. *Some Days I Flip My Lid* by Kellie Bailey (2019) is also great. You can use it with children of all ages, and it pairs well with *The MindUP Curriculum* because the concept of a flipped lid is taught in both. Consider weaving that instruction into the health curriculum so that it is sustainable. But if the teachers are not giving the lessons themselves, make sure they and all staff members learn about healthy limbic system development and the need for regulation throughout the school day.

Countless regulation tools are available, and one size definitely fits one here—there is a regulation tool for everyone. Some of the tools that seem to work for many include glitter wands, silicone sponges, putty, pinwheels, and puzzles.

- **Glitter wands** should be at least 12 inches long. The short ones don't allow enough time for the liquid to shift. Students can make their own glitter wands, just be sure that the liquid is thick enough to allow for slow movement of the contents.
- **Silicone sponges** are meant to be used in the kitchen. They are also antimicrobial and soothing when held between your hands or rubbed on your arm or leg. I have also had students who put them in their mouths. If you have never seen a silicone sponge, search for it on the internet. They are easy to clean and can also be individually assigned, particularly for students who prefer to put them in their mouths.
- **Coloring** is one of the most widely appreciated regulation tools. Some people can focus for longer if they are coloring. Some students like to draw or doodle. If you are concerned that they are not attending to the lesson, tell them about your

concern. Read a paragraph while the students are coloring or drawing and ask them to retell the story. You may find that many students have better auditory retention and comprehension when they are coloring, drawing, or doodling. You may occasionally find a student who does not focus while coloring. That student should look for another regulation strategy. Some students change tools based on the circumstance.

- **Spinners** were originally marketed to parents of children diagnosed with ADHD. I have found that the spinner serves as a stimulant. Children who have an excessive need to move, tap, and wiggle are probably better served with tools that tend to sooth and relax. Some students like one tool in the morning and another in the afternoon. Some of my middle school students are big fans of spinners in the morning because they are stimulating. Often, they use coloring or silicone sponges in the afternoon.

- **Pinwheel breathing** (or "yoga breathing" or "calming breath") is a free and uncomplicated regulation tool that we all carry with us; thus, you can use it anywhere, anytime. I use a pinwheel here because it really helps children regulate their breathing, and it's fun to watch the wheel go around. Invite the student to sit up with their feet planted on the floor. (This can also be done standing.)

  Draw attention to their breath by asking them if they can feel that their inhalation is cool inside their nose. Establish an inhale and exhale number. Breathe in through your nose and fill up your belly and chest until you cannot fit any more air. Count as you do this. Then double your inhale number by controlling your exhale through your mouth. We all have different inhale numbers based on our size, lung capacity, and speed of counting. Demonstrate pinwheel breathing by inhaling through your nose and exhaling through your mouth using your inhale and exhale numbers. Direct the exhale at the pinwheel. You may want to invite younger children to place their hand on their belly so they can feel their inhale and understand how to fill up with air.

Regulation tools should be readily available in the classroom and, thus, their proper use should be explicitly taught. If a student is not using a tool correctly, model it and make your expectations for its use clear. These are not toys. They are tools with a designated use, just like Chromebooks, rulers, and protractors.

Designate a place in the classroom where students can excuse themselves from their desk and work on regulation. At times students may become so dysregulated that they need a smaller and quieter place to regulate. Discuss this ahead of time and make a plan for where they can go. If you find that a student uses the need to regulate as a way to escape the classroom, try to find out why the student is so eager to be away. What is in the way?

Introducing regulation tools into the classroom and teaching students about their limbic system is proactive and preventative. Leaving the classroom to regulate is reactive. Either way, regulation tools will increase task perseverance, improve attendance, and, over time, increase academic outcomes for all students.

Executive Function Instruction

In Chapter 2, we explored the effects of childhood trauma on the development of executive function capacities. Typically, early childhood classrooms explicitly teach children how to develop many of the executive functions. As the grade levels increase, often the explicit instruction for executive functions decreases. Increasing the capacity for executive functions may help to keep students from being referred for special education services. (More about this in Chapter 4.) Let's revisit those capacities from Chapter 2 and consider some strategies for encouraging their development and increasing academic performance for our students.

Attention

Direct the attentional processes, including filtering interference, attention to task, and the inhibition of impulsive calling out. How many times have you asked children with impulsivity to pay attention? I'm guessing your answer is something like "too many" or "too many to count." In the early stages of limbic system development, attention is not a choice. If you work with middle or high school students, you may be assuming they should know how to pay attention. If their development is delayed, they might not have the same ability as their peers to choose to attend. Use regulation tools to increase attention and decrease sensitivity to sound and touch stimulus.

Judgment and Task Organization

Initiate judgment about the amount of time or effort that a task requires or understanding how to approach an assignment. This might be why some of your students avoid starting an assignment or why they start and then give up in frustration. You might see it as a behavior problem if you know the student has the cognitive ability to do the work. Imagine how frustrating it could be to think you understand the lesson and then become overwhelmed or confused by the assignment.

Conference with students who struggle with task organization. Ask them to discuss their approach to the assignment. Model strategies for breaking the assignment down. Create a quick and simple flow chart they can follow. Keep in mind that sometimes in our effort to help students approach or organize their ideas, we create graphic organizers that seem to the student to be just as difficult as the assignment. Keep it simple. As you discuss how a student might approach an assignment, illustrate what you discuss. You may need to create an illustration for each assignment until the student begins to grasp the process on their own.

Have you ever asked a 2-year-old to build a complicated starship with LEGO bricks? Probably not. Have you ever tried to get a 2- or 3-year-old to clean up? Possibly you sang a song and cleaned along with them, until they gave up and walked away after picking up one or two items. You cleaned up the rest of the room yourself but were pleased that the child participated in the activity. Now think about an assignment you gave recently. Would a 2-year-old be able to complete it? (Never mind about reading ability. I'm referring to the child's perception that they could accomplish the task.) I bet you are thinking "why would I give this 4th grade assignment to a 2-year-old, Melissa?" Exactly! You wouldn't. And yet, you give grade-level assignments to students with the executive capacity of a 2- or 3-year-old every day.

Consider that children who are avoiding work, participating in distracting behaviors, or aggressively refusing to work are operating on the perception that the assignment is impossible and that it will take forever. If the student thinks an assignment will take too long, use a timer to show them what their actual pace of work is. Often, they grossly underestimate their abilities. You may need to break the assignments down to meet the student where they are, then build up the student's belief in their own abilities over time. Operating on the assumption that "they should be able to do this" will only interfere with the overarching approach of "how can I help you?" If this capacity has not developed by the later years, it must be explicitly taught.

Processing Speed

Regulate the speed of information processing—auditory or visual. Students who struggle with visual processing speed often have difficulties learning to read. Students with auditory processing speed issues may struggle with lecture format. This is a good place to remind you that superior teaching is trauma-informed teaching. Make an effort to be sure that you use a visual illustration of most of what you say. Always provide a visual illustration or depiction of any new vocabulary. Write the words on the board and provide pictures that match. Smartboards and multimedia have really made it easy to provide visual and auditory blended instruction. If you are doing a lecture, particularly in the upper grades, be sure that there are opportunities for students to turn and talk with each other. You can also break up a lecture format with activities that students work on individually or together. This will give a student with a processing speed delay an opportunity to catch up and be sure they stay abreast of what is going on in the class.

Multimodal Teaching

All students benefit from multimodal teaching. Note the modalities you employ to teach content over the course of the week. I'm talking about your instructional strategies, not the activities the students complete. Do you cover visual, auditory, tactile, and kinesthetic? At the elementary level, you should cover all four in the course of a day or two. Middle school teachers should cover all modalities in the scope of two to three days. High school teachers should cover them over the course of a week.

- **Visual.** How often do you support what you say with a visual representation? Visually represent what you are saying as often as you can. This can be a picture, a chart, a graphic organizer, or notes of the lecture. Microsoft PowerPoint is one useful tool. Be sure that your slides have pictures and labels. Avoid lengthy paragraphs.
- **Auditory.** Do you talk for more than 10 minutes at a time? The length of time you talk without pausing for student interaction should be commensurate with the age of the children you work with. Consider the following guide:
    - 3–5 years old: 5 minutes
    - 6–8 years old: 10 minutes
    - 9–12 years old: 15 minutes
    - 12–25 years old: 20 minutes

If you teach 4th grade, be aware that you have students in your class with the processing speed of 2nd, 3rd, 4th, and 5th graders and vary your pauses accordingly. Keep in mind that pausing for student interaction can involve asking a question or doing a quick pair–share. It can be brief. Children with auditory processing delays may need to receive a copy of notes or a recording of the lecture that they can go back through slowly. Avoid assuming that students are not trying or are not paying attention. Regulation tools, especially coloring and doodling, can greatly improve auditory processing speed.

- **Tactile.** So often in our work we feel pressure to cover content and move through the curriculum. This pressure often results in lecturing, giving an assignment, and moving on to the next topic. We need to talk less and have the students do more. In addition, as students move through the grades, they have fewer tactile learning opportunities. It's common to see sand trays, rice trays, and artistic renderings of understanding through the clever use of noodle art in kindergarten and sometimes into 1st grade. But it is possible that less than half of the students in any classroom have developed age-appropriate processing speed by the end of 1st grade. Teachers in upper elementary through high school should keep asking, "How can I include touch in this lesson?" This is a great opportunity to blend differentiation with regulation. If you are providing regulation tools in the classroom you can often pick them up and use them as instructional tools to go along with what you are talking about. Sometimes the touch—particularly in a secondary classroom—is not necessarily touching of the content, but keeping that sense engaged throughout a lesson.
- **Kinesthetic.** Activities that feature movement are typically found in kindergarten and 1st grade classrooms, but by 3rd grade, teachers exhaust themselves just telling kids to sit down. Flexible seating is a great way to allow for movement

while learning. Let your students lie on their stomachs on the floor, lean up against a bookcase, or sit in a bean bag chair. This works not only for 5-year-olds, but for all of us. Ask students to arrange themselves into the four corners of the room in response to prompts as a way to review previous learning. Or ask for thumbs up or thumbs down if they agree or disagree. Instead of asking for raised hands, invite your students to stand up if they think the day's date is an odd number. Dance in all forms is excellent teaching. I am no dancer (yoga is about my limit) but it doesn't matter. If you are not comfortable with dancing, just move around the classroom. Play a quick game of Simon Says using your content. I do this in my work with adults in professional development. It's great fun and increases attention and deepens understanding by increasing processing speed. Again, regulation tools would be useful here as well.

Working Memory

Directing the ability to hold and manipulate information. Students who struggle with working memory often ask you to repeat directions. These are the "Wait. What?" kids. An example of this is when you provide two- or three-step directions verbally to your class. You might even ask for a student to restate the directions you just gave. The class gets to work, and somebody says, "Wait. What?" Take care not to assume that the student was not paying attention. Maybe they were; maybe they were not. The point is to give the benefit of the doubt, just in case they were paying close attention and their brain is struggling to store information so that they can use it again. That's what we do when somebody gives us two- or three-step directions. We have to hold on to the first two directions in order to process and make sense of the third direction. You can support and improve this executive function capacity by providing visual representations and limiting auditory presentation of multistep directions.

Middle school and high school students may need to be supported with modifications. As we move into the middle and high school years, instructional practices become more auditory and less visual—although teachers who use a variety of multimedia opportunities are improving this traditional practice. As we see more and show less, some of our students with working memory challenges begin to struggle and fall behind. This is an opportunity for a well-crafted IEP to support these students. The IEP can include modifications for the general and special education teachers regarding delivery of content for students with working memory issues. Basically, it can be anything from visual representation of key terms to providing everything of importance that is said in a class in a visual manner. However, if we all endeavor to explicitly address working memory (and really any of these capacities) through the curriculum we are already teaching in the earlier grades, we will be able to drastically reduce the number of middle school and high school referrals to special education.

Consider Jude. Jude is a 6th grader whose teachers have noticed that he does not pay attention and that he struggles with multistep directions. A quick conversation with the teachers reveals that they know he doesn't pay attention because he never knows what is going on in class. When a teacher gives directions, the class gets started, and, inevitably, Jude will call out, "Wait. What? What are we supposed to be doing?" One teacher explained, "I give Jude an individual explanation. He goes back to his seat and still doesn't know what he is supposed to do." After a discussion with Jude's teachers about working memory, they noticed that when they work one-on-one with Jude and ask him to repeat what they say, he is often unable to do that. When they began giving him written directions and visual depictions of the lesson, his participation and engagement improved immensely.

Long-Term Memory

Direct the efficient placement of information. Students might be able to take in information and understand its meaning, but their long-term memory function doesn't know where to store it (and thus be able to recall it). Admittedly, long-term memory and information storage is a more complicated issue than some of the others. Some students benefit from instruction in the use of mnemonic strategies. Many need much repetition and strategies for providing that repetition for themselves as they move into high school. Word boxes, open note tests, and fill-in-the-blank questions are much better ways to determine what a student with long-term storage issues knows.

Writing

Direct the collaboration of multiple abilities to produce written responses that represent the level of their understanding. Writing is a complex neurological and emotional activity. Writing has been linked to self-regulation and self-efficacy (Bruning et al., 2013). *Self-efficacy* is a student's perception of their potential for successful completion of a task or skill. Students with DT often have a delayed sense of self (Schore, 2009).

Consider students in kindergarten. They do not typically have a firm sense of what they do well and what they need to improve. By the time those students are in 5th grade, they are starting to know who they are, what they like, and what they do not like, and they are gaining some understanding of their strengths. A child with DT is delayed in that progression. In addition, they may have fragile attachment and a perception that they are unworthy or no good. The delay in development of self and the negative self-perception interferes with the writing ability in children with DT.

Students with trauma need teachers to provide safety and attachment (remember our CARES framework). Meet them where they are. If they give you one sentence, take it today and get two sentences tomorrow. Conferencing with students about the writing topic, organizing information into parts, and making an outline are all ways that students can be taught to extend their writing. Start by accepting a bulleted list if that's what your student is able to give. Creating safety, connection, and regulation often results in more writing and more creativity of content. The process of writing can improve the delays caused by trauma.

Sense of Humor

Counterintuitive though it may seem to talk about trauma and humor, laughter really is the best medicine. Countless studies have examined the health benefits of laughing (Lovorn, 2008; Neuhoff & Schaefer, 2002; Soloman, 1996). It has been shown to reduce blood pressure and increase the release of oxytocin, a hormone that helps with empathy and trust (Neuhoff & Schaefer, 2002). Humor in the home and in the classroom builds trust and increases engagement in learning (Lovorn, 2008).

We all benefit from humor in our lives. Find ways to laugh each day. In one of the schools where I worked, we instituted a joke of the day. It started as a part of the morning announcements. But to develop agency and connection, we started a joke club. That club then started providing jokes to classrooms. Some teachers had students provide a joke throughout the day. We had an observable improvement in attitude and a measurable decrease in discipline incidents that year. In addition, I noted an increase in staff attendance.

A Trauma-Informed Behavior Response

The CARES framework works for behavior as well as learning. In fact, you really should not separate the two. When behavior improves, learning improves. When learning improves, behavior improves. Let's return to our discussion of Iggy from Chapter 2. Iggy's teacher was trauma informed, followed the CARES framework, and this is what actually happened.

After the first time that Iggy took off running through the building, his teacher met with her principal, counselor, and colleagues. First, they shared everything they knew about Iggy. The counselor was aware of his separation from his mother. His teacher knew that his grandmother was his legal guardian. Next, they counted up the ACEs (more than three) and realized they were dealing with a child of trauma. Finally, they created a plan to build attachment and create safety so that Iggy would be able to stay in his classroom despite the noise, distraction, and interpersonal challenges. When Iggy took off, someone would cover the class, and the teacher would go down the hall and let Iggy know she was there (building attachment slowly). It was important that the teacher do this, not another member of the staff, so that Iggy could build a relationship and create a feeling of safety in class. She did not chase him, and she did not threaten him. She just stood at an intersection of the hallways so that he could see her when he ran by. She was careful to maintain a neutral expression on her face. She did not glare at him disapprovingly, nor did she use this as an opportunity to tell a joke. She remained calm and patient. Then she would move down the hall toward her classroom when he was looking at her. He would run past and get to the classroom first or follow not too far behind.

Over time, Iggy would stand in the doorway when he became stressed, but he would not leave. He was becoming attached to his teacher. She became safe to him. Then the teacher set up a "keep-calm" corner. Iggy moved in. He was in the corner all day, but he was not disrupting the class, picking on classmates, or running out of the room. He was not doing a lot of schoolwork, but the teacher suspected he was listening.

Accept approximation. Students cannot learn if they are running through the halls. They cannot learn if you respond to the running with exclusion. Keeping Iggy in the classroom was the first goal. Next, the teacher worked on encouraging some learning. Once in a while, he would work one-on-one with the teacher on an assignment. Then, he began participating in class discussions from his corner. The teacher moved his guided reading group to a table next to the corner. Iggy was listening. He ended the school year spending half the day in the corner and half the day with the class. He was much calmer. He was also on grade level in most academic areas.

The plan for Iggy was proactive and reactive. Certainly, something had to be done when Iggy would bolt from the room. But they also made a plan to reduce and eventually extinguish the behavior. Iggy learned to feel safe because his teacher did not scold him or make him feel bad about himself. The classroom was organized and followed a daily routine. Iggy began to embrace the routine and was quick to tell his teacher when things did not go according to plan, thus demonstrating a sense of agency. Iggy was given the opportunity to slowly build a connection with his teacher. The keep-calm corner allowed Iggy a place that was not as stimulating. The class also learned about their limbic system throughout the year. Iggy learned along with the rest of the class how to regulate and communicate his needs. The curriculum provided the teacher with a framework for teaching Iggy how to learn, and in return, he learned to access some of his executive function capacities.

The CARES framework is effective for older students, as well. Consider Dallas. Dallas is a high school student who lives with his mother and his older sister. (His parents are divorced.) They live in a large home in an affluent part of town. His mother is an engineer with a large beverage company. The police have been called to the home numerous times. When Dallas was younger, his mother would call the police and ask them to take Dallas away because he wouldn't listen to her. When Dallas was 12, he called the police and reported that his mother was intoxicated and abusing him.

His elementary school teachers would describe him as charming, but he could also be a "little devil." Academically, he was capable but inconsistent. When he was engaged in an activity, he did well across all content areas. Meetings with Dallas's mother yielded little result. She would blame the school and was often heard saying things like, "He's a nightmare. I should have never had him. If you think you can do better, you take him."

Dallas's middle school teachers would describe him academically as lazy. His attendance became sporadic in 7th grade. He failed language arts and was written up for lying, stealing, and cursing at staff. He would occasionally become aggressive and toss a chair and leave the classroom. His mother lost her job and often missed meetings, sometimes calling a day late to reschedule.

In high school, Dallas's attendance continued to be sporadic. He was inconsistent academically. In 9th grade, he received As for all marking periods in math, art, and physical education. His language arts grades varied from A to F to C to B. He grew close to his art teacher and would often eat lunch with her while working on projects. He helped her set up for the art show, sometimes staying after school for hours. His work was featured that year in the district art show. At home, his sister was arrested during a loud party at the home where she was intoxicated and in possession of a large amount of prescription pills. The art teacher left on maternity leave in November, with Dallas failing art in the subsequent two marking periods. He did well in language arts, but almost failed math for the year. His attendance continued to be sporadic. He missed four or five days per month and was often tardy on the days he did attend.

When Dallas was in 10th grade, his father was granted custodial guardianship. The counselor, school social worker, assistant principal, and three of Dallas's teachers, including the art teacher and his math teacher, met as a team to make a plan for Dallas. Some states require an intervention team or student services team to meet to discuss a student who is struggling with behavior or academics. In many cases, this is a precursor to any involvement by the child study team and a special education referral. In some places, this is not a requirement in the response to intervention (RTI) framework or a multitiered system of supports (MTSS), but it is recommended. (I'll discuss RTI and MTSS in further detail in Chapter 4.)

The staff shared what they knew about Dallas's experiences. His father was able to add some detail and verify some events. The team agreed on an ACE score of eight. Note that this ACE score is really a starting place that helps to determine the extent of childhood trauma exposure. You need not spend a great deal of time making sure you have the exact number. It is even common to have some disagreement among the team regarding the exact number of ACEs.

After a review of Dallas's past, he was invited to join the meeting, and the team briefly reviewed the state of Dallas's high school progress with him. This is a good opportunity to think about the amount of shame Dallas feels, but it helps to briefly and objectively state where things stand. At this point, simply accept whatever Dallas says to confirm or deny and move along. Avoid a power struggle at all costs.

The entire team, including Dallas, created an action plan that followed the CARES framework. A morning check-in with the counselor would help establish a feeling of safety. They would discuss how Dallas was feeling and what he wanted to accomplish during the school day. Regular interaction with the math and art teacher would encourage connection. Dallas agreed to join a photography class after school. The school social worker met with Dallas a few times to teach him about his limbic system and to create a plan for regulation as needed throughout the day. The math teacher reinforced executive functions. Dallas seemed to have language and memory capacity, but he struggled with task organization and time management. The team agreed to meet again six weeks later. He occasionally missed photography club and meetings with his math teacher. Each time, one or both of the teachers followed up. Dallas's attendance improved, and his grades slowly became more consistent. By graduation, Dallas had earned a 2.85 grade point average, was highlighted in the senior art showcase, and had plans to attend community college.

Patience with the process is what unites these two case studies. All too often, we fall back into the trap of applying a consequence, carrying out the sentence, and moving on until someone notices that the same student continues to need consequences and no improvement is occurring. The CARES framework takes teamwork and time. Children are unique—no two plans are ever exactly the same. The framework is effective for children with and without trauma exposure. It's about building relationships and resilience, things we want for all our students.

Applying the CARES framework across the curriculum, in general education and special education settings, may decrease the number of referrals to special education. It may also increase the number of students who are declassified or who receive all their IEP services in a general education setting. One size fits one, however. Despite all our efforts, there will always be students who need an individual approach in our schools. That is why it is of the utmost importance to develop trauma-informed IEPs that support the CARES framework and the trauma-informed practices taking place in the school at large.

4

Crafting Trauma-Informed IEPs

Like traditional individualized education programs (IEPs), trauma-informed IEPs follow the Individuals with Disabilities Education Act (IDEA) procedural safeguards and your state's administrative code. You write them using the same templates. But a trauma-informed IEP considers the trauma experience of the student. In a trauma-informed IEP, the effects of that trauma can be evident in any one or all three standard areas of evaluation (the learning assessment, the psychological assessment, and the social history). In addition, the CARES framework as a means of addressing the student's needs is evident in the modifications and program sections.

Remember, however, that creating trauma-informed teachers and staff doesn't start with the IEP. If your evaluation team is writing trauma-informed IEPs, it is important that your school has a plan for teaching the entire adult school community about the effects of trauma on learning and behavior. Students with IEPs are in the PE class, the art class, and the music room; they are in the cafeteria and on school buses. Many students receive their programs completely in the general education classrooms. Everyone in the school is a part of IEP implementation. As such, everyone needs to understand

Staff education first before IEP

73

childhood trauma so that they are better prepared to implement the trauma-informed IEPs your team creates.

As I've mentioned, most of my professional years have been spent in the northeast, where most states have what we call a child study team (CST). The team comprises a school psychologist, a social worker, a learning disabilities teacher or consultant (LDTC), a general education teacher, a special education teacher, parents or guardians, and, when appropriate, the student. I will be referring to the special education evaluation team as the CST, even though not every state has an LDTC or uses this term for their evaluation team. Each state has its own administrative code that establishes the finer points of procedure and due process that is outlined in the federal IDEA. With a little bit of creativity and flexibility, all the ideas and suggestions in this chapter can be carried out legally in any state. Trauma-informed IEPs are legally defensible IEPs.

A New Look at Some Old Identifiers

Let's take a look at something most of us do not control but all of us have to live with: diagnoses for mental illness. Typically, members of a CST are not medical doctors and, thus, do not provide students with medical or psychiatric diagnoses. Many of us have had to incorporate diagnoses into IEPs and Section 504 plans, however. It is not within the scope of our profession as educators to challenge, change, or dismiss medical or psychiatric diagnoses provided to us by the medical community and passed to us by parents and guardians. We can, however, look at these identifiers with our new trauma-informed lenses.

Experts are working to establish developmental trauma (DT) as a medical or psychiatric condition (van der Kolk et al., 2005). The assignment of a diagnosis in the big book of recognized psychiatric disorders, the *Diagnostic and Statistical Manual of Mental Disorders* (DSM; American Psychiatric Association, 2013) requires a tremendous amount of peer-reviewed research, money, time, and political persuasion. In the meantime, DT is a recognized condition that indicates childhood exposure to adverse experiences. Formal recognition of developmental trauma disorder (DTD) has not yet been accepted by the American Psychiatric Association, which is responsible for updating and revising the DSM. But the concept of DT is recognized in research and by many doctors and psychologists (van der Kolk et al., 2009). The suggested definition for DTD will require a new understanding and possible revision of current diagnoses, including ADHD, bipolar disorder, depression, anxiety, oppositional defiance disorder (ODD), intermittent mood disorder (IMD), and reactive attachment disorder (RAD). It is not for me to say whether these conditions will be changed or deleted before or after the addition of a definition for DT. I am not a medical doctor, and I hold no licensing credentials. What follows is based on research, my own decades of personal experience, and my professional experience training and consulting on this topic.

The neurobiological effects of childhood trauma can manifest in learning and behavior that can look much like other things. Many children with DT are hypervigilant or hyperaroused. They can struggle to filter out unimportant sounds. They can appear impulsive and hyperactive. The large quantities of cortisol, adrenaline, and other toxic stress hormones that may be flooding their systems can initiate freeze, flight, and fight behaviors. Their hyperarousal can look a lot like and is often misdiagnosed as ADHD. Also, as a result of an overactive amygdala and toxic levels of hormones, children with DT can have excessive mood swings. They can appear to be depressed, anxious, or, in some cases, vacillate their mood to the extent that it mimics bipolar disorder. Children with DT often struggle with attachment and interpersonal relationships. They might have difficulty trusting adults. They may, as a result, confront persons in authority. They may resist adults telling them what to do—for example, in the cafeteria or on the bus. They can appear oppositional and defiant. Such an overlap exists between the characteristics of ODD and DTD that some

Overlap of Characteristics of ODD & DTD

believe that ODD is actually an early and incomplete recognition of DTD (Cook et al., 2005).

The point of looking at these identifiers through a trauma-informed lens is that in many cases, regardless of the diagnosis a team receives, a trauma-informed IEP can reduce and occasionally eradicate the symptoms of the aforementioned conditions in a student who has experienced trauma. We must also recognize the potential for comorbidity. For example, a child genetically predisposed to depression can also have DT. The label applied to a condition is not as important as what we as educators do to support learning and behavior in schools. A trauma-informed approach can greatly improve student outcomes and, at the least, will not harm anyone.

Identifying Trauma in the Data

We can write trauma-informed IEPs for newly classified students and after an annual review. For the purpose of this discussion, we will assume that the student is a new referral to the evaluation team. The road to writing a trauma-informed IEP, as with a traditional IEP, starts with data collection to determine if evaluation for special education services is appropriate at this time.

Background Information

Before we begin a discussion of the IEP process, it's pertinent to discuss what happens before we sit down at a table to determine eligibility for special education. Some states require a tiered intervention process that can lead to a referral to special education. Many school districts have some form of a tiered intervention process, whether it is required by their state or not. Some places call this the response to intervention (RTI) process and some refer to this as the multitiered system of supports (MTSS) process. Both processes involve a tiered intervention system in place in the schools. Tier 1 refers to general education and is what I call "good for all." The curriculum is a Tier

1 program. Things that all students have access to without question belong in Tier 1.

Tier 2 refers to opportunities that are available to students in general education but with some criteria for entrance into the program. Tier 2 is what I call "good for some." A good example of a Tier 2 program is a remedial reading program. Some students get an additional dose of reading throughout their day or a few times a week. They may meet in small groups with a teacher who is different from their classroom teacher. In middle school and high school this could be a separate class.

Tier 3 is typically where we find special education. Tier 3 is what I call "good for few." Tier 3 interventions are generally available to the fewest number of students in your school. They are highly specialized, can be expensive, and may have additional funding streams. As mentioned in Chapter 3, some states and districts require an intervention or student support team to discuss a student and develop and carry out an action plan prior to any referral to special education. In some schools and districts this is a recommended approach, maybe not required. For the purposes of this chapter, we will assume that the students who are referred for a special education evaluation, and potentially for the development of an IEP, have already been through some form of a tiered intervention approach.

What do we know and what can we find out about a student who has been referred for evaluation? The process begins with a meeting where the team reviews the data and asks questions of the adults in the school who know the student well. What strategies for learning and behavior are already being employed? Here, the team would review any documents created during the RTI or MTSS process and examine formative data such as report cards, attendance, health records, tests, and recent assignments. For students in middle school and high school, take the time to review information from elementary school.

How many places has the student lived? Are there inconsistencies in grades across content, marking periods, or years? Children with trauma histories often struggle with relationships. As such, they may perform well in a class with a teacher with whom they feel safe or connected. Conversely, despite high math aptitude, that same student might do poorly in math the following year. Are they frequent flyers to the nurse's office, often without any specific medical condition? Sometimes children with DT are seeking a connection and the nurse is in a quiet space. Sometimes, they are seeking to avoid challenges they are having in a class or with a teacher or peer. Children with preoccupied attachment styles will seek out the nurse or counselor more often than a child who is securely attached. These are things that we need to know before we begin the testing. Knowing about attachment and possible trauma exposure may change what we observe during testing.

Consider Evalina. Evalina was a 14-year-old 9th grader in a large public high school. She was referred to the CST for consideration for special education because she was struggling across many academic areas. At the time of her referral, Evalina had been in five different schools districts in three states. She was living with a foster family after child protective services removed her from her birth mother for the third time. Her school attendance was inconsistent, and she was often late to school when she did show up. Almost every day that she was in school, she spent a minimum of 30 minutes with the school nurse. She had been written up for cursing and was suspended twice for disrespectful behavior and leaving class without permission.

During testing, Evalina would swing between being cooperative and engaged and seemingly distracted and tuned out. She was polite and smiled frequently at the evaluators. The person who administered the learning evaluations reported that Evalina was engaged and worked well for about 45 minutes. After that, she needed frequent breaks. The school psychologist who administered the psychological evaluations reported that she was charming and willing to cooperate. He reported that at first her behavior was not at all an issue during testing. Then he mentioned that a fire drill occurred between sections of the assessment, and upon returning from the evacuation, Evalina

Student cooperative. Therefore
drill — resistant & stopped trying
Trauma Informed IEP would stop testing
for the day.

Crafting Trauma-Informed IEPs 79

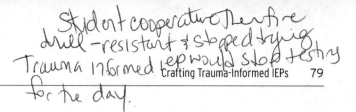

was resistant and stopped trying. She told the evaluator that she was tired and didn't want to work anymore. He was able to complete the testing anyway. When asked if the school psychologist believed that the disruption of the fire drill affected the score, he indicated that he believed his scores were accurate. He believed that Evalina was just being coy and that she knew what she was doing.

Time for that paradigm shift. Evalina's history with and frequent separation from her mother and her numerous homes and caregivers would indicate that at the very least, Evalina has fragile attachment and childhood trauma. Evalina was triggered by the loud noise and mass movement that occurred during the evacuation for the fire drill. She was not able to regain regulation and therefore was trying to flee the testing environment. The school psychologist should have discontinued testing for the day when the fire alarm sounded. Trauma-informed IEPs consider the when, where, and how of the testing environment. The regulation and feeling of safety for the student being tested is more important than anything else. Students with trauma need to feel safe, be connected, and get regulated before and during testing for special education evaluation. If they are not, the scores may not be accurate.

During the initial data review and before administering testing, *Student Map for initial data review* consider using a student map (see Figure 4.1 for an example focused on a student, Brianni, whom we'll discuss in detail later in the chapter) to provide information to the CST to better understand the whole child they are considering for evaluation. Conversations with teachers and parents can also help the team provide an appropriate testing environment that is calm and safe.

The Testing

Tests should comprise three basic areas of assessment: psychological, learning, and social. Evaluators have many well-known assessments available to them to collect information about a student in each of these three areas.

FIGURE 4.1
Student Map

Name: Brianni

Date of Birth: 4/5/2012

Grade: 3rd

Teacher: Mrs. Sunshine

Student's Strengths: (academic, social-emotional, extracurricular, resources)

- Likes interacting with people
- Cheerleader
- Excellent dancer
- Supportive father (mother currently incarcerated)
- Has good ideas for writing
- Healthy
- Good attendance

What does the student say?	What does the student think/feel?
• "No one likes me." • "I'm no good at learning." • "I hate math." • "Mrs. Sunshine does not like me." • "I'm always in trouble." • "I love to dance and cheer." • "I didn't do it."	• She has no friends. • She is lonely. • She doesn't like school.
What does the student do?	**What are the student's 3 wishes?**
• Walk around the room or move constantly. • Interrupt others when they are speaking. • Start a task but not complete it. • Blame others. • Steal things from classmates. • Bother classmates.	• To have friends • To be good at school • To dance on Broadway and have my father watch

Describe the Parent Concerns: (Father)

I want Brianni to do well in school. She needs to try harder. I have a lot of trouble getting her to complete homework. Every time I look up, she has left the table and is off doing something else. I have to work nights sometimes, and I am sure she doesn't do her homework. She stays at the neighbor across the hall when I work nights, and my neighbor tells me that Brianni doesn't mind her at all. I know she misses her mother, but we don't talk about it.

Teacher Concerns:

Brianni is constantly moving around the room. She bothers the other students when they are working. During group work, she takes control but doesn't understand the activity. She can be bossy. She causes problems with anyone who tries to befriend her by lying. She is bright but doesn't apply herself. She struggles with reading and math, but I'm not sure if it's the content or the fact that she rarely pays attention. She frustrates easily, gives up, and won't try again. Her father will occasionally attend meetings about Brianni. He does not answer emails.

Data Review:

√ Report Card Summary (Attach 2 most recent report cards): She received three *C*s in reading, writing, and math. She earned a *D* in social studies and a *C* in science. She earned an *A* in physical education and a *B* in art. She failed Spanish.

√ Standardized Test Score Review: Partially proficient in Grade 2 test in both ELA and math.

√ District Summative Assessment Review: Started but did not complete the fall district writing assessment. Scored a 77% on the fall district math assessment.

√ Review recent work samples from each core content area (Attached): Handwriting is neat but small. It gets larger and messier as she becomes frustrated. None of the assignments are completed.

Conclusions:

Goal/Action/Plan:

Follow-Up Meeting Date:

Psychological Evaluation. The most common assessment in this area is the *Wechsler Intelligence Scale for Children* (WISC-V; Wechsler, 2014). The WISC-V generates a full-scale IQ score, which comprises five primary index scores: verbal comprehension index, fluid reasoning index, working memory index, and processing speed index.

The verbal comprehension index measures a child's overall ability to verbally reason. This subtest may be influenced by semantic knowledge—a representation of the scope of words a child knows and can use in a spoken or written sentence. Children with DT may have language development delays and thus may have a semantic knowledge base that is from one to three years below their chronological age. In addition, it has been shown that children who live in lower socioeconomic status (SES) homes have a smaller semantic knowledge base than children in middle SES and above homes (Perkins et al., 2013).

Because of the complex intersection between language development and trauma exposure, it is essential that children are tested in their first language. For children who may have lived in the United States for a few years, an interview with parents can help determine the child's primary language. Does the child continue to speak their first or native language fluently at home? Can the child read or write in their first language? If the interview indicates that the child's learning language is English but the child still speaks their first language at home, then the test should be administered in a combination of English and the native language. The child should be encouraged to speak and write in either language.

The fluid reasoning index measures a child's inductive and qualitative reasoning. This index includes orally administered math word problems. Children with working memory delays or an immature semantic knowledge base might score lower in this subsection. (Note: None of these subtests is designed to stand alone, and there is crossover in all of them. The brain is a highly complex organ.)

The working memory index measures a child's working memory by repeating lists of numbers in ascending and descending order.

Younger children look at pictures and try to recall the pictures they saw in the correct order. Older children listen to spoken numbers and letters and repeat them in a predetermined order. This score may be affected by attention. Children with DT can feel dysregulated because they do not know the assessor, they have never had this type of assessment, or they are terrified that they will not perform well. Although this assessment has been created to mitigate these external factors, the effects of trauma on the parts of the brain engaged in these activities is unique and complex.

The processing speed index measures the speed at which a child can get tasks done. Children with DT may have an interesting inconsistency here. More often than not, I have seen a very low processing speed that seems inconsistent with other scores and is lower than it should be in relation to the overall score. This discrepancy could have a number of causes, but the most common is what I call "playing chess in a hurricane." Imagine you are outside in a dangerous hurricane. I invite you to sit down and play chess with me. You might tell me I'm out of my mind and run to safety. You might try to play but feel like you can't think because you are so worried about the rain, wind, lightening, and thunder. Children with DT have signals in their brains that are making them feel like they are in the middle of a dangerous storm. Some take longer than typically developing children to complete tasks or provide responses to questions because they have to fight through the storm in their head.

The WISC-V contains five additional subtests that can help shed light on inconsistencies in scores in the original five indices, as they seek to further divide capacities such as working memory. The auditory working memory index, for example, specifically targets auditory memory and separates it from the visual memory engaged in the working memory subtest.

Learning Evaluation. The two most common assessments of learning ability are the Woodcock-Johnson Tests of Achievement (Schrank & Wendling, 2018) and the *Wechsler Individual Achievement*

playing chess in a hurricane

WJ

Test, Fourth Edition (WIAT-4; Wechsler, 2020). Both tests measure reading, math, written language, and oral language.

All too often, I've seen students receive the barest minimum of subtests. The learning consultant or assessor of academic achievement may feel the pressure of a case load that is too large. Team members in collaboration with teachers may feel that the learning issues are obvious and thus extensive administration of subtests is not warranted. But inconsistent scores on subtests are common with children with trauma, and I strongly recommend that the learning evaluation contain the administration of as many subtests as needed to make sense of discrepancies and inconsistencies. Consider giving the subtests from the WIAT-4 if the Woodcock-Johnson is the primary, for example. Administering a cross-section of subtests will often shed light on the data and provide the team with specific information that will adequately inform the development of learning goals and necessary modifications. Administering a more than adequate number of subtests across the two tests will provide highly accurate information on any child, with or without trauma.

The *Behavior Assessment System for Children, Third Edition* (BASC-3; Reynolds & Kamphaus, 2015) is a multidimensional system used to assess the behavior and self-perceptions of children and young adults. This assessment has a teacher rating system, a parent rating system, and a student self-report. Use this system with extreme caution. The BASC-3 language does not incorporate an understanding of the neurobiology of trauma. The phrasing of the questions implies choice on the part of the student. Scores can imply consideration of conduct disorder or ODD but no consideration of the effect of a hyperaroused amygdala on behavior. If you administer the BASC-3 to a student with a trauma history, you must consider the effect of trauma on the development of the limbic system.

The *Behavior Rating Inventory of Executive Function* (BRIEF; Lutz et al., 2004) is an assessment of executive function capacities at home and at school. This assessment includes questionnaires for parents and teachers, self-reports for adolescents ages 11–18, and a preschool edition. As previously discussed, children with DT can have delayed development of any of the executive function capacities because many of them are connected to development of the hippocampus. Administered in conjunction with the WISC-IV and the Woodcock-Johnson, BRIEF can provide an expansive view of a student's strengths and weaknesses.

Social Evaluation. The interview for social history is where the team can collect specific information regarding a student's experiences. The social history should be conducted by a school social worker who has been trained in ACEs. As schools become trauma-informed communities, they should also conduct parent informational sessions. As previously discussed, every adult involved in the school community, including parents, should be informed about ACEs. Offer sessions multiple times throughout the school year at different times of the day, including a virtual session that can be recorded and posted to the school website. If your school has conducted these sessions, then the social worker can ask parents during the interview if they know their own ACE score. That question can lead to an invitation to complete a survey on behalf of their child. Keep in mind that an ACEs survey completed by parents on behalf of the child is only an estimate. ACE scores are highly dependent on an individual's perception of events. It is impossible for a survey completed by parents to be completely accurate. It does, however, serve as a point of reference. You can include this assumed ACE score in the report.

If your school hasn't conducted community meetings about ACEs, then the social worker should embed some of the questions from an ACEs survey in the interview. Remember that there are an infinite number of ACEs in the world. Take care not to get too hung up on the original 10 ACEs (see Chapter 1). Explore the potential for intergenerational or cultural trauma. Ask about the family's socioeconomic status. Consider the geographical location of the family. Has there ever been a traumatic environmental event such as a hurricane or tornado that threatened shelter or food securities? Do not include this assumed ACE score in the report if the parents are not familiar with the concept. The team, however, should proceed with a trauma-informed IEP if the social history or informal data review shows potential for the student to have been exposed to three or more adverse events.

Related Services

Speech and Language Evaluations. It is common practice to pass on speech testing if the student does not exhibit any articulation challenges. Many children with complex childhood trauma are challenged by receptive and expressive language delays, age-appropriate perspective taking, and social cueing. A trauma-informed evaluation should include the linguistic, pragmatic, and narrative aspects of language.

Occupational Therapy Evaluations. The developmental delays commonly associated with childhood exposure to trauma can include delayed vestibular development. This can be the case even if the student does not exhibit any outward signs of gross or fine motor delay. Most of the assessments typically administered by a trained occupational therapist can yield evidence of this delay if that therapist is trained in the neurobiology of trauma. In addition to identifying developmental delays in fine or gross motor skills that may be evident with a traumatized child, these evaluations can highlight the need for accommodations and modifications, like regulation strategies, and a calm and nurturing learning environment.

The Language of Trauma-Informed IEPs

Trauma-informed language should be evident in the IEP document and ingrained in how educator teams discuss children with IEPs during planning, implementation, and follow-up. For instance, general and special educators must avoid deficit-based language, such as saying a child *won't* do something, as opposed to saying a child *can't* do something. A trauma-informed educator understands that all

avold deficit language

children would if they could, and this understanding must be clear in how educators write and talk about the children they support. A student who is not behaving or performing academically as expected is not being defiant or manipulative but has something in their way. Teachers must also be mindful of trauma-informed language when completing PLAAFPs (present levels of academic achievement and functional performance) or PLEPs (present levels of academic performance). All too often, present-level summaries read like a catharsis on the part of the teacher. Their frustration is evident in their choice of words. They blame the student for "choosing not to practice the strategies that were taught."

Here is an example of a traditional present-level summary written by the classroom teacher, using the student featured in the student map in Figure 4.1. (Note: Some PLEP forms have a breakdown of academic areas, and some include social emotional sections. For this example, all areas will be combined into one section.) Brianni is a 3rd grade student with between six and eight ACEs. She lives with her father. Her mother left the family for incarceration two years prior and has not had any contact with Brianni since she left.

> Brianni continues to struggle with following directions. When asked to complete an assignment, she will shake her head or say "No." She only completes what she wants to complete regardless of what is required. After initial refusal, she complies with directions 50 percent of the time. On two occasions, Brianni pushed a chair over. On both occasions she eventually picked up the chair and apologized for her behavior. In addition to chair throwing, Brianni demonstrates frustration by tearing up worksheets or attempting to leave the classroom. When she leaves the classroom, she is always told that leaving the classroom is not respectful behavior and that there will be a consequence. In response to this comment, she frequently curses at me or at our classroom aide. She comes back to the classroom immediately 40

percent of the time. Brianni will not work with class peers on assignments. She demands to work alone. When she does work in groups, she will take the lead even if she does not understand the activity. Currently, Brianni works in groups 30 percent of the time.

Brianni is working in a 3rd grade math curriculum. She has demonstrated proficiency in addition, subtraction, and regrouping in addition and subtraction. She does not know her multiplication facts beyond the 3 times table. She can use a calculator with proficiency and is on track to master basic currency calculations. Brianni can complete word prob-lems when she applies herself. She attempts word problems 20 percent of the time. Word problem completion accuracy is at 90 percent.

In the area of reading, Brianni is reading on Level C, an early 2nd grade level. Brianni walks around the room frequently during reading. She is reluctant to read out loud. Her lack of attention has caused a delay in her reading skill acquisition. With effort, Brianni can read beginning 3rd grade text. She will not try without 1:1 support in reading.

Note the use of language that implies that Brianni could respond differently if she wanted to: *"She only completes what she wants to complete regardless of what is required. After initial refusal . . . ."* and *"Brianni will not work with class peers on assignments. She demands to work alone."* The text does not mention that her trauma has affected her academic ability or behavior.

This is also an instance where cultural competence can come into play. In this fictional case study, it bears mentioning that Brianni is Black and Mrs. Sunshine is white. As you increase your won cultural competency, you may start to notice patterns. As I learned more and spoke to people far more knowledgeable than myself in the area of conscious and unconscious bias, I started to note that some of the performance reports I was reading, written by white teachers, used more accusing language for their students of color than for their white students. I mention this here mainly as a type of pattern to be mindful of. I have also read many performance reports written by white teachers regarding Black and Brown students that did not indicate unconscious bias.

Now, let's look at Brianni's present-level summary written with trauma-informed language.

Brianni demonstrates behaviors that are consistent with fragile attachment, fear of abandonment, and hypervigilance. Multistep directions challenge her limited working memory. Brianni responds well when multistep directions are provided visually and when assignments are broken down into manageable segments. She completes activities with multistep directions with 80 percent accuracy.

Occasionally, Brianni will refuse to complete assignments or follow directions. Brianni needs an opportunity to get regulated before she can have a conversation about her concerns for completing a task or following directions. Brianni is initiating self-regulation activities 50 percent of the time, and she will comply with requests to use or access regulation tools 80 percent of the time. Brianni's task completion rate when she is regulated is 90 percent. Currently, Brianni does not feel safe when working with peers on assignments. She is provided with the opportunity to work alone. When she chooses to work with her peers, she struggles to maintain control. Brianni would benefit from continued support with small-group interpersonal skills.

Brianni is working in a 3rd grade math curriculum. She has demonstrated proficiency in addition, subtraction, and regrouping in addition and subtraction. She does not know her multiplication facts beyond the three times table. When she sings the times tables, she has a 75 percent accuracy rate through the seven times tables. She can use a calculator with proficiency and is on track to master basic currency calcula-tions. Brianni can complete word problems when she is reg-ulated. She attempts word problems 20 percent of the time without an opportunity to work with a trusted adult. With a trusted adult, she completes word problems 100 percent of the time. Word problem completion accuracy is at 90 percent.

In the area of reading, Brianni is reading on Level C, which is an early 2nd grade level. Brianni exhibits hypervigilance and flight behavior during reading. She is reluctant to read out loud. Brianni will read out loud with fluency with the support of a trusted adult. Since we have welcomed a class-room aide into our community, Brianni has made strong progress in reading. Her comprehension skills are on target to reach grade level by the end of the year. Brianni would benefit from strategies to strengthen her attachment and decrease her dependency on adults to complete assignments she perceives to be difficult.

In the trauma-informed sample, the teacher mentions Brianni's fragile attachment and her need to develop skills to increase independence. There is no mention of chair throwing, and it seems that the teacher is spending time helping Brianni get regulated and become indepen-dent with the strategies. As a result, Brianni is not pushed to the point where she explodes and throws chairs or leaves the room. Brianni appears to be making better academic growth in a room where she has felt safety and regulation.

Provide training and a sample PLEP written in trauma-informed language to help teachers and team members who contribute writ-ten information to the development of an IEP. Ongoing coaching and discussion are helpful as IEP authors learn to communicate the social-emotional and academic levels of students with trauma. And consider that trauma-informed PLEPs can be written for any student, with or without trauma. All children benefit from connection, a feel-ing of safety, and regulation. Many children with or without learning challenges become dysregulated and can experience low self-esteem and self-efficacy. Regulation strategies and a caring and patient adult can contribute to an overall improvement in achievement and self-esteem.

Trauma-Informed Modifications and Accommodations

The modifications and accommodations section of an IEP is where the team can list strategies and opportunities that a student will need to find success in the classroom. Some IEP templates do not distinguish between modifications and accommodations. Some only address accommodations as they relate to standardized testing. Modifications are often considered to be strategies that level the playing field for children with unique learning challenges. Accommodations are changes in the way information is presented. Regardless of the way your template organizes this section, consider differentiating between process, product, and content.

Process is the way the student takes in the information. Is it verbal, visual, written, performed, and so on? Product is the way a student shows what they know. For example, does the student write the information, speak their thoughts, use a graphic organizer, or make a diorama? Content is the scope and sequence of the curriculum that is presented. What is being taught to the student? Is it the same content being provided to all students in the grade level? Is the content reduced or simplified? Some IEP templates separate this section between special education and general education settings. Whether the sections are separate or not, the environment where learning takes place should be considered. Students may need certain strategies in PE that they do not need in an art or math class.

Educator teams writing trauma-informed IEPs should consider process, product, content, setting, and the CARES framework when selecting accommodations and modifications for students. What follows are suggestions for modifications that address these categories and that, where possible, align to the CARES framework. Keep in mind that any number of modifications and accommodations are possible. The only limit is your imagination and the needs of the student.

Process Modifications

- Listen to audio recordings instead of reading text. Even better, listen to the story and follow along in print.
- Learn content from audiobooks, movies, videos, and digital media instead of reading print versions.
- Consider the physical appearance of the test on the page of a worksheet, quiz, or test. Make sure your assignments are well-spaced and organized. Technology advancements make this easier and more accessible to educators. You can find examples of well-spaced worksheets, tests, and quizzes on Pinterest and many other educator websites.
- Provide text in a larger print size. Even students with glasses who may not have an IEP will benefit from large print. Consider purchasing a few large-print versions of the books or texts you use in class that are not already in electronic form.
- Have a designated reader—someone the student knows—read the text on tests and quizzes aloud. Relationship to the reader is important here. The student should know and be comfortable with the reader. Try to keep the reader consistent so that this person might become a trusted person in the student's school life. Students benefit from both hearing text read aloud as well as reading to themselves. The designated reader should be an adult, not a fellow student. (Safety)
- Make sure students can hear instructions spoken aloud. The student needs to be in a place free from auditory distraction and competition. A voice amplifier can be effective for some.
- Record lessons. This strategy is most effective in the higher grades. Make sure the student has been taught to how to organize the information when they listen to it later either through notes or a graphic organizer.

- Allow students to share notes. Make this practice as casual and common as possible to avoid embarrassment or stigma associated with asking for help.
- Provide an outline of your lessons. Many learners benefit from knowing where the lesson is going from the beginning. Students who struggle to stay focused during a lesson can find their place in the content if they have an outline.
- Use visual presentations to accompany oral delivery of information, such as word webs, PowerPoint presentations, and anchor charts.
- Provide instructions in written form. All students will benefit from your providing written instructions for tasks and assignments, especially in high school.
- Allow students to listen from the classroom regulation station or keep-calm corner. They may need extended time in the regulation space. Avoid calling them back to the general seating because you are moving on in a lesson. (Regulation)
- Allow students to color, doodle, or draw while listening. (Regulation)
- Provide a variety of visual and tactile tools for students to use during lesson delivery, such as glitter wands and silicone sponges, and allow students to choose what helps them regulate in the moment. (Regulation)
- Modify activity lengths as needed (e.g., provide 5 math problems instead of 20). Meet your students where they are. Whether you teach 2nd or 8th grade, if a student is successful working on one problem independently before giving up, checking out, or finding other ways to entertain herself during the activity, then start there and add on as the student shows the ability to persevere.
- Provide flexible seating. (Regulation, Safety)
- Allow students to move around the room frequently. (Regulation)

Product Modifications

- Give responses in a form (spoken or written) that's easiest for the student. This may vary by content.
- Dictate answers to a scribe who writes or types for the student. This could be an inclusion teacher or possibly the person who reads tests and quizzes. If this is needed daily and throughout the lesson, then an aide should be assigned. (Attachment and Connection)
- Capture responses on an audio recorder. Students may be self-conscious about this one. Be sure to provide a space to work that does not interfere with the other students (e.g., have headphones for every student).
- Use a digital spellchecker. Google Docs and Microsoft Word make this easier and more common. Students who struggle to spell will often resist writing because they are afraid they will not be able to spell the words they want to use to communicate their ideas. Consider teaching the student to use a speech-to-text tool. It takes training to be able to speak your thoughts in an organized fashion. Have you ever tried to write a paragraph using the speech-to-text option? Try it. It will help you assist your students. Start small. One sentence at a time.
- Use a computer or word processor to type notes or give answers in class. (Executive Function)
- Use a calculator or table of "math facts."
- Create a diorama or pictural representation, write a song, or perform a play as an option for completing an assignment.
- Sit the student near a trusted adult while working. (Safety)
- Provide a regulation station and give access to regulation tools while working. (Regulation)
- Create a strategy for organizing each assignment (e.g., time, layout, what to do first). (Executive Function)

- Set individual due dates and time for task completion. Collaborate with the student and adjust as time goes by. (Executive Function)
- Use goal setting throughout the school year to help develop time management and improve task completion and assignment engagement. Goals can be long-term ("By the end of the school year I will . . . ") or short-term ("Tonight I will compete five problems on my math worksheet." or "This week I will complete my vocabulary sheet and write a paragraph.") (Executive Function)
- Allow for noise-canceling headphones while working. (Regulation)
- Provide the option for the student to work independently during group work. If students are uncomfortable or unsuccessful working in a group, allow or encourage them to work alone and build up to working with a partner and eventually a group. It's OK if it takes the entire school year to develop the skills necessary to work with three or more partners. (Safety)
- Modify test questions to match executive function capacity. Often, you will have students in your class who are reading below the grade level you are teaching. For example, if a student struggles with language, use words that are as concrete as possible. You can run your word documents through a Flesch-Kincaid grade-level test (several versions are available online for free) to check for alignment with a student's capacity. (Executive Function)

Content Modifications

- Teach memorization strategies. (Executive Function)
- Focus on unit goals.
- Provide instruction in native language. (Attachment and Connection)

- Provide materials that are at the student's reading level. General education and special education teachers should work together to compile resources for students, especially those reading more than two grade levels below grade level. Many websites and apps can provide education materials commonly used in a standard curriculum. Fountas and Pinnell have an extensive library of levelled books. This is a great opportunity for choice. Give the student several appropriate books to choose from.
- Provide instruction in social skills. Classroom teachers should work with the school psychologist or school counselor. This is another great application of *The MindUP Curriculum*. (Attachment and Connection)

Setting Modifications

- Adjust lighting to levels conducive to learning for the student. You can use flame-retardant shades to cover your fluorescent lights to soften the light. (Regulation)
- Incorporate small-group work and instruction. Some students benefit from learning new content in a small group. Some students can acquire the content in a large group but need review time in a small group. (Attachment and Connection)
- Provide an alternate lunch space for a student to get away from the busy cafeteria. This is a great idea for *all* students and should be open to anyone. The space should be smaller than the cafeteria (possibly a classroom that is empty during lunch) and should have its own rules and expectations surrounding its use. It is *not* a place that should be used to make up missing work. Students may self-select to complete work while they are in there, but no student should be required to do so. If a teacher needs a student to miss recess or spend lunch time making up work, then the teacher should be responsible for the supervision. Otherwise, consider creating an additional lunch duty position to provide supervision or ask for parent volunteers. It

may take some time to find a space, provide supervision, and teach students about how to use the alternative space, but the lack of time you spend on post-lunch or recess drama will be worth the initial investment. (Regulation, Safety, Attachment and Connection)

Most, if not all, of the modifications in these lists are good for all students. Educators should strive to create a classroom community where everyone gets what they need, with or without an IEP. These types of classroom communities help all students feel accepted and free to access any tools necessary for learning. Headphones are one example. They are excellent for noise canceling, audiobooks, soothing sounds, and more, and they should be available for all students in your classroom. Students should not be embarrassed or ashamed to access learning tools. And you should *always* make sure students know why they benefit from these modifications. When students have the opportunity to understand their modifications, that contributes to their agency. Be sure to explain to them in a way that the student can understand based on their age.

IEPs and Student Behavior

Most IEP templates have a section for a behavior improvement plan (BIP). Complete this section and attach a BIP to the IEP document as needed. One of the most dramatic paradigm shifts required on the journey to trauma-informed education might be the movement away from behavior modification practices. The BIP in a trauma-informed IEP should include not a point sheet or sticker chart but a plan for regulation and attachment developed in collaboration with the parents and the student. The plan should include a goal and data collection. Chapter 5 will further explore the need to shift from cognitive behavior practices and examples of trauma-informed behavior plans.

Most IEP templates also include a section regarding adherence to the school's discipline policies. As previously discussed, exclusion, suspension, and detention can be harmful and biased. Until the school district gets to the place in its trauma-informed journey where the school board amends the policies that support exclusion, trauma-informed IEPs should exclude the student from all policies involving suspension or exclusion, except when it comes to weapons or drugs. A student who brings a weapon to school needs to leave school property, and schools must follow their local and state laws regarding weapons. A student who brings drugs into the school or comes to school under the influence of an illegal substance should be removed from school property and taken to the appropriate medical or psychiatric facility. CST members can use research on the neuro-biological effects of trauma on development as justification for the modification of adherence to school policy.

Training and Support

Trauma-informed IEPs are the product of a trauma-informed process implemented by a team of trauma-informed professionals. Schools should make every effort to educate parents and guardians on the effects of adverse experiences on child development. It's just as crucial for the teachers implementing trauma-informed IEPs and providing modifications to be able to recognize the effects of trauma on development and to have opportunities to learn to respond in a trauma-informed way. A trauma-informed IEP, once developed, can only be carried out by educators who have had the opportunity to learn about the effects of trauma on neurobiological development and who have had training in the CARES framework.

This training and support can't be limited to just special education teachers, either. Children who receive special education services are in many general education settings as a part of their school day. And you cannot trauma-inform a school from the IEP out. The teachers who are responsible for providing special education services are immensely talented, but they don't do this alone. A rising tide lifts all ships. Schools need to elevate the teaching capacity of *all* the educators in the school by providing them with research-based professional development that helps them improve their instruction and thus increase the learning capacity of all students.

5

The Trauma-Informed Functional Behavior Assessment

The 1975 Education for All Handicapped Children Act (Public Law 94-142) ensured that all children were provided a "free and appropriate public education" in the "least restrictive environment." In 1990, the U.S. Congress amended and reauthorized PL 94-142 as the Individuals with Disabilities Education Act (IDEA). This revision included language regarding school personnel response to behavior that interfered with learning. School personnel were required to collect data and implement programs designed to improve behavior. The functional behavior assessment (FBA) was born. In 2004, further revision to IDEA included language regarding tiered intervention. Response to intervention (RTI) has taken on many forms throughout the ensuing years. Positive behavior intervention and supports (PBIS) and multitiered systems of support (MTSS) outline schoolwide systems for leveled intervention. Many schools now employ behavior specialists who are trained to collect data using FBAs.

Exploring the Traditional FBA

The FBA is a process for assessing the purpose or function of a student's behavior in relation to environmental stimuli so that appropriate interventions can be developed. It is a formalized procedure involving multiple observations, analysis of the data, development of a hypothesis, and administration of an intervention. Collecting information and developing a program based on the collected data has long been a successful approach to any intervention.

The FBA is based in applied behavior analysis, which is derived from behavior modification theory (B. F. Skinner, 1974). Behavior modification theory explains behavior as a response to environment. Learned behavior can be improved or changed through operant conditioning. Operant conditioning involves adjusting the probability that a specific behavior will occur in the future by adding or removing one of two basic types of stimuli: positive reinforcers or negative reinforcers (M. E. Skinner & Hales, 1992). As a result, plans developed using a traditional FBA often seek to improve the perceived problem behavior by providing positive and negative reinforcers.

Many educators see behavior as a choice. In fact, many of us were taught that behavior is a choice because, as previously discussed, our preservice education programs have been largely based on cognitive and social learning theory. As a result, we see behavior as something we are motivated to do in search of a desired result—almost premeditated, if you will, although not always consciously. I'm not convinced that a 3-year-old who is on the floor kicking and screaming because someone took his lollipop has a predetermined understanding of the outcomes of his behavior. He may know, however, that kicking and screaming does get mommy to attend to him.

Let's remember Iggy from previous chapters. A traditional view of Iggy's decampment from the classroom would be that he is attention seeking. He is running out of the classroom either because he is (1) avoiding work in the classroom, (2) trying to get the teacher's attention, or (3) a bad kid and doesn't have any manners. We now know, however, that Iggy had a number of adverse childhood experiences in his young life. His amygdala and ANS were wired for protection against perceived threats. His hippocampal and prefrontal cortex development was delayed. He was in flight for his safety. His brain thought he was protecting himself from the threats in the classroom. The potential threats were many. He may have feared relationships with other students. He may have been concerned that he would not be successful academically. He may have felt threatened by the potential for a relationship with his teacher. My guess is that it was a combination of all those things.

What we haven't discussed is that Iggy's teacher was originally given a behavior plan. A team conducted a traditional FBA, collecting baseline data on the number of times Iggy ran out of the classroom and had other disrupting classroom behaviors. They established that his motivation was attention seeking and avoidance. His behavior chart would indicate his rewards for time spent at his seat doing his classwork. For the first two days, Iggy was excited about his behavior plan. He was engaged and focused on his acquisition of stickers—so much so that one might see his focus on the acquisition of stickers as an obsession. On the third day, Iggy left his seat and went to the doorway. He stood in the doorway smiling at his teacher, and then he started to walk down the hall. Then he came back to the door and peeked in, smiling. He then ran down the hall, and it took almost an hour to get him to return to class. When he realized he would not get a sticker because he left his seat and left the classroom, Iggy had a full-scale meltdown. He was kicking and screaming and crying and inconsolable. He did not understand why he did not get a sticker. Things continued to get worse until a new counselor explained a more relationship-based response to Iggy's teacher.

The behavior plan that incorporated external rewards and consequences only served to increase Iggy's feelings of worthlessness and hopelessness. Think about it. Adverse childhood experiences are outside of children's control. They are not things that children do, but rather things that happen to them. A behavior plan is something that the adults in the school do to a student. Giving rewards or taking away privileges can increase students' sense of loss of control and increase their perception that they are not safe, thus thwarting the development of agency. When children do not feel safe, they might withdraw or act out. Research is now suggesting that children who are not doing what they should be doing based on teachers' predetermined set of expectations are *unable* to do so (Porges & Carter, 2017; Schore, 2009; Siegel, 2012; van der Kolk et al., 2009). The student's challenging or disruptive behavior is a symptom of a larger issue (Porges & Carter, 2017). All behavior is a form of communication. Acting out or withdrawing are signals that a student is not getting something they need. Our challenge is working with the student to figure out how to identify and meet that need.

In addition, implementing BIPs requires a great deal of time and expense. Teachers need to track and record points and purchase rewards. Many teachers express concern that they do not have time to manage the behavior plan. As a result, they maintain the plan inconsistently, thereby increasing the student's feelings that they have no control over their environment and furthering their feeling of distrust (Greene, 2018). For those who are reading this and thinking, "I use behavior plans and they work," consider how many times plans are forgotten or lose their effectiveness. You may make short-term gains, but transferring responsibility for behavior from the adult awarding points to the student is tricky. Long-term improvement is rare and often makes the problem behavior worse over time (Rowan et al., 2020).

Adding the Trauma-Informed Lens to the FBA

The traumatology framework crosses over behavior modification theory in that a student's behavior might be more a response to stimuli than a premeditated choice. However, the traumatology framework expands the concept of environmental influences to include past events that affect the child's ability to accurately process the environment. Thus, a trauma-informed FBA (TIFBA) considers what has happened to the student and seeks to build improved behavior through regulation and relationship.

The TIFBA is meant to replace the traditional FBA. You can use it as a data collection tool in the initial IEP development or in the event of a new and challenging behavior problem after the IEP is in place. You can also use the TIFBA to develop a Section 504 plan. Many schools use the FBA as a part of the RTI process.

Like a traditional FBA, the TIFBA is designed to identify, target, and treat specific behaviors. With a TIFBA, however, the theoretical framework shifts from a behavior modification base to an attachment and traumatology framework. The strategies are designed to change behavior from the inside out rather than the outside in (e.g., from looking at behavior as being "attention seeking" to an invitation to respond). The TIFBA draws strategies from the CARES framework; the objective is to create safety, agency, regulation, and executive function.

The overall process of conducting a TIFBA is consistent with that of a traditional FBA.

1. Collect background information on the student.
2. Define the problem.
3. Devise a plan to collect data. You will need a minimum of three observations of 60 minutes before you can develop a program.
4. Compare and analyze the data.
5. Formulate a hypothesis.
6. Develop SMART (specific, measurable, achievable, relevant, and time-bound) goals and write the plan.
7. Implement the plan.
8. Monitor progress. Implement the TIFBA plan for a minimum of three weeks before scheduling a review meeting.

The TIFBA action plan provides teachers with strategies and processes to follow and templates for data collection. The TIFBA action plan should include strategies for how general education, inclusion, and special education personnel will work together to carry out the TIFBA and a plan for supporting the student based on the results.

Let's return to Brianni. A meeting between her father, her classroom teacher, and the school counselor might produce the information in the sample student map in Figure 4.1 on p. 80. A school psychologist or behavior interventionist would conduct three observations at different times of the day on different days (anyone who understands how to objectively log behavior could do so, but these are the best suited to the task). Figure 5.1 outlines one such observation session, with detailed time stamps, observations, and notes.

FIGURE 5.1
A Sample Trauma-Informed Behavioral Observation

Name: Brianni **Date:** 3/1/20	**Trauma-Informed Behavioral Observation**	**Observer:** M. Sadin
Timed Increments	**Observed Behavior**	**Notes**
2:00–2:05	Upon return to the classroom from art, Brianni moved around the room.	
2:05–2:15	Colored with me. The conversation was disconnected. She changed the subject four times.	
2:15–2:20	Walked away from the coloring table and toward the computers. Invited by the teacher to work at the pattern station.	Class in transition from math mini-lesson.
2:20–2:30	Worked on the pattern activity with the paraprofessional.	
2:30–2:35	On the floor at the pattern activity table, she made six or seven screeching sounds. Paraprofessional asked her to stop. She screeched three more times and threw pattern materials.	Class in transition to next activity
2:35–2:40	Was directed to the computer station by the teacher. Ran across the room to the computer station. Pushed a boy out of the way and grabbed the laptop computer away from him.	
2:40–2:50	Put the laptop down and started the activity. When she finished the program, she slid the laptop to the boy.	

continued

FIGURE 5.1 (*continued*)
A Sample Trauma-Informed Behavioral Observation

Name: Brianni Date: 3/1/20	Trauma-Informed Behavioral Observation	Observer: M. Sadin
Timed Increments	**Observed Behavior**	**Notes**
2:50–3:00	Found a book on the table and slid it in front of the screen, blocking the boy from seeing the program. Did this three times. Paraprofessional asked her to stop. She continued three more times.	
3:00–3:05	Moved to the pattern station and interfered with another student's work by placing her body between student and the materials then sliding the materials across the table away from the student.	Class in transition to next activity
3:05–3:10	Invited by the teacher to work with her in a small group. Worked with the teacher.	
3:15–3:25	She left the small work group with the teacher. Went and stood by the door for two minutes then went to the pattern table. Engaged another student with similar behavior to previous time at the pattern table.	
3:25–3:35	She crawled around on the floor by the cabinet. The paraprofessional asked her to stop. She continued. The paraprofessional engaged her in a conversation about her assignment. She began talking loudly, insisting that another student wrote on her work. She packed up her backpack, walked around the room, screamed when another student attempted to use a marker she had been using earlier, and grabbed the markers from the student and put them in the box in her cubby.	The class was directed to clean up their stations and pack up for departure.
3:35	She walked to the bus with her classmates.	

© 2022 Melissa Sadin

In addition to helping the team discover what has happened to Brianni, the informational meeting also helps to prepare the observer to see Brianni's behaviors through the appropriate lens. Note the language the observer used to describe the behavior. For example, "On the floor at the pattern activity table, she made six or seven screeching sounds. Paraprofessional asked her to stop. She screeched three more times and threw pattern materials." This observation simply notes the behavior with no language to imply that it was attention seeking or premeditated. Another example from the observation is, "Moved to the pattern station and interfered with another student's work by placing her body between student and the materials then sliding the materials across the table away from the student." Again, the sentence is completely objective. The observer was looking for attachment style and signs of dysregulation.

After collecting and analyzing the data, the team creates the TIFBA plan, which includes background, a summary, target behavior goals, current interventions, and implementation strategies (see the Appendix on p. 111 for a sample completed plan). The strategies should target three tiers of intervention. In the case of Brianni, her class had not yet learned about their limbic system, so one Tier 1 strategy involves doing so. Teaching the whole class about the limbic system will help Brianni feel included. There may not be an opportunity for a Tier 1 strategy for every child. Some children are receiving their services in a more restrictive environment. Sometimes, the lack of strong classroom management on the part of a teacher can increase hyperarousal in a student like Brianni. A TIFBA can provide for global improvement in classroom management, which would benefit all the students. Some teachers who implement a TIFBA action plan learn some trauma-informed strategies that they then apply to other students.

A Framework for the Future

Teacher training and professional development are crucial to the success of a TIFBA. The person responsible for conducting the assessment should be fluent in traumatology and the effects of trauma on attachment, learning, and behavior. Schools need to develop long-term plans to create a trauma-informed school community.

Research about adverse childhood experiences has been available since 1997. It is no longer brand-new information. It is time for the paradigm shift. It is time to incorporate research-based, evidence-based, well-established science into our practice. We must evolve. When we grow and learn, our systems and processes often follow. We are *required* to provide the children of this country who've been identified as having disabilities and a need for specially designed education and intervention with a free and appropriate education. It seems to me that "appropriate" in this context means "in keeping with research and evidence-based practices."

In 2014, the Substance Abuse and Mental Health Services Administration (SAMHSA, 2014) put forth a framework for creating a trauma-informed organization. The framework—known as "the four Rs" (realizing, recognizing, responding, and resisting retraumatization)—is certainly applicable to schools and the process for writing trauma-informed IEPS.

We must **realize** the prevalence of trauma. Start with what has happened to a student before we attempt to properly analyze any data collected on a student. IDEA requires that a social history be taken as a part of the initial data collection process. We already recognize that a student's social history must be considered when crafting an individual special education plan for a student. It is time to update our process to include recent research on child development.

We must **recognize** the effects of trauma on the neurobiological and psychological development of children. All educators teach children with special education needs. All educators must receive adequate professional development on the effects of trauma on learning and behavior. This is not a one-and-done program. Rather, becoming trauma-informed is like becoming culturally competent or becoming a master teacher. It is a journey, not a destination. It requires scaffolded and continuous training and focus. When all educators in a school have the opportunity to learn about trauma, they will be more prepared to provide a trauma-informed community.

We must **respond** in a trauma-informed way. In our profession, that means trauma-informed instruction and behavior response. Research shows that trauma-informed instructional strategies and processes improve academic outcomes for all students (Phifer & Hull, 2016). You may also notice a reduction in referrals for special education evaluation as trauma-informed and trauma-focused instruction takes root in your school. When students with mild learning challenges have access to multimodal and differentiated instruction year after year, they will grow and expand their executive function capacities and have greater access to their natural cognitive abilities.

And finally, and possibly most challenging, we must **resist retraumatization**. Retraumatization is a conscious or unconscious reminder of past trauma that results in a re-experiencing of the initial trauma event. Retraumatization is often triggered by a situation, attitude, expression, or environment that replicates the loss of power, control, and safety that occurred with the original trauma. Most ACEs are outside of the student's control. For example, a student who lives with a parent struggling with substance abuse does not possess the ability to stop the parent's addiction.

Too often, educators feel great pressure to stop inappropriate behavior, dispense a consequence, and run off to the next fire. Thus, we neglect to include the student in our thinking and decision making. We do things *to* students, not *with* them. This can look and feel a lot like the lack of control students have over their adverse experiences. Administering the TIFBA can help to include the student and the student's past experiences in the data collection and the plans for the student. Data collection for a trauma-informed IEP is about starting with what has happened to the student. When we see the data and the student through a trauma-informed lens, then we can create an individualized program that is appropriate for the student.

I have always believed that when you tell the educators, you change the world. One educator has access to many parents. Evaluation teams are uniquely poised to inform parents about the effects of trauma on development. Providing trauma-informed individualized education and whole school programs will help to heal children of trauma. Now that you have made it to the end of this book, you are on your way. Go change the world!

Appendix
Sample Completed Trauma-Informed Behavior Intervention Plan

Student: Brianni

Date of Birth: 4/5/12

Date of Report: 3/15/20

School: Sunnyside Elementary School*

Developed By: Melissa Sadin

Background

Brianni is a 3rd grade student at Sunnyside Elementary School. An interview with her father indicated that she has been exposed to three confirmed adverse childhood experiences, two of which are ongoing. Her father reports that her mother has been in prison. Brianni has been to the prison to see her mother. Brianni's mother was released from prison recently, and her whereabouts are unknown. Brianni's father has a fiancée that is not Brianni's mother. He has an infant daughter with the fiancée. Brianni's father and his fiancée have come to the school to meet with Brianni's teacher regarding Brianni's behavior at home. The fiancée sends Brianni to her room for time out when she does not comply with parental requests.

Brianni scored in the below-proficient range on her most recent standardized test. Her most recent report card showed an *A* in art, *A* in physical education, *B* in science, *D* in social studies, *D* in math, *D* in literacy. Her teacher commented that "Brianni is capable of the work when she applies herself" and "Brianni is easily distracted."

Brianni reports that she does dishes and other household chores to help her stepmother. She said her teacher was "OK." She reported that she "doesn't really like school" but

---

* School name is changed.

she "likes to see her friends." When asked if she has difficulty staying in her seat, she explained that her father tells her she has "ants in her pants," so she "doesn't like to sit still." Her three wishes were to get better grades, to have more friends, and to dance on Broadway.

Summary of Observed Behaviors

Brianni demonstrates hyperarousal and insecure attachment. She was observed showing an exaggerated amount of physical movement. During one-on-one and small-group lessons, she moves from concept to concept every six to eight seconds. Brianni demonstrates a need to form exclusive relationships with the adults in the room. She displays social-emotional behaviors of a typical 3-year-old. She becomes extremely agitated during transitions from activity to activity in the classroom and when moving to another location in the school. She is able to sit in a chair and participate in a minilesson for about five minutes. She is able to color and listen to a classroom minilesson or a story being read aloud. She is able to remain engaged in a computer program for 10 minutes. She responds positively to pinwheel breathing.

Trauma-Informed Behavior Summary

After a complete review of the data, the presence of hyperarousal and fragile attachment is confirmed. As a result of exposure to adverse childhood experiences, Brianni is demonstrating social-emotional behaviors similar to those of a 3-year-old child. These predominantly hyperactive behaviors are a result of neurobiological stimulation in unstructured environments. The toxic hormone release causes Brianni to become physically active, and she can be aggressive with peers during this hyperarousal. In addition, her behaviors are interfering with her ability to learn.

Target Behavior

(*Dysregulated behavior demonstrated by a child who has been exposed to adverse childhood experiences is caused by neurobiological responses to identifiable and unidentifiable environmental or biological triggers.*)

The target behavior is hyperarousal triggered by unstructured times in the classroom.

Baseline Data Collection Date(s)

2/25/2020, 2/28/2020, 3/1/2020

Baseline Average

Six occurrences of dysregulated behavior in six opportunities for transition.

Plan Objectives and Goals

A decrease in hyperarousal behaviors will indicate improved relationship development and may indicate an increase in resiliency. As Brianni learns to regulate her reaction to stimulating environments through the intentional use of mindful behaviors, she will be able to respond in a more age-appropriate manner. She will also be more available for instruction.

Current Interventions

Brianni is placed with a teacher who has a working knowledge of the effects of trauma on development, behavior, and learning. Brianni has been provided with a safe place in the classroom. She is encouraged to sit in a chair during carpet time and is permitted to color during times of dysregulation. She also has a classroom paraprofessional in the class 80 percent of the day.

Recommended Interventions

Brianni requires opportunities to develop trust with key adults and peers in her school environment. In addition, she would benefit from strategies to develop resiliency. *(Resiliency is defined as the ability to demonstrate self-regulation, personal agency, and inoculation in response to stressors.)*

Tier 1 Strategies

1. Classwide implementation of *The MindUP Curriculum*.
2. Classwide use of *The MindUP Curriculum* language in classroom rules and expectations.
3. Classwide instruction in the pinwheel breathing technique.
4. Conduct transitions in an organized way with no more than four children moving at one time.
5. Restructure center time to provide weighted choices for all and some purposeful grouping that allows for specific data collection.
6. Immediately upon return to the classroom from lunch and recess, engage the class in calming activities such as listening to a read aloud story or Brain Gym.
7. Play soft music during classroom work sessions and center time.

Tier 2 Strategies

1. Continue unrestricted use of the safe space.
2. Prompting to use the pinwheel breathing technique when signs of stress are demonstrated.

3. Develop with Brianni's implementation team a list of relationship-building prompts to encourage her participation in classroom instruction. Such prompts should include

   - I noticed your effort on this.

   - Let's work together to understand this information.

   - It seems that this work is challenging you. How can I help?

   - I noticed that you are out of your seat a lot today. Do you need more regulation opportunities?

   - I noticed that you have not started on the activity. What is in your way? How can I help?

   - Your behavior is interfering with the learning of others right now. We all need to feel safe in this classroom. How can I help you to feel safe and allow others to return to their work?

4. Have Brianni participate in a small social skills group with the school counselor.

5. Twice per week, engage Brianni in one-on-one instruction with her teacher.

6. Provide Brianni with guided adult supervision during all classroom transitions.

Response to Target Behavior

When Brianni demonstrates inappropriate classroom movement, an adult should encourage her to participate in either some time in her safe space, coloring at a table by herself, or pinwheel breathing. Provide lavish attention when she agrees to participate in one of the mindful activities. Adults should model expression of thoughts and feelings while using one of the mindful activities. "Can you feel yourself relaxing?" "Can you feel the breath coming in your nose?" "Can you feel the expansion of your belly?" "How do you feel now that you have done a breathing activity?" Use a calm and regulated mood and tone with Brianni at all times. Give constant acknowledgement of the choices she makes, good and bad, without shame.

Indicators of Success

1. Brianni will comply with requests to participate in mindfulness activities 80 percent of the time.

2. Brianni will demonstrate appropriate classroom behavior during transitions 100 percent of the time.

3. Brianni will demonstrate at least one age-appropriate peer interaction per day (e.g., sharing, waiting her turn, listening to a classmate, showing compassion or empathy, helping a classmate).

4. Brianni will increase her participation in classroom instructional activities to three content areas.

Brianni's Relationship Team: Classroom teacher, paraprofessional, school counselor.

Behavior Plan Review Date: 3/25/2020

References

Alink, L. A., Cicchetti, D., Kim, J., & Rogosch, F. A. (2012). Longitudinal associations among child maltreatment, social functioning, and cortisol regulation. *Developmental Psychology, 48*(1), 224–236. https://doi.org/10.1037/a0024892

American Psychiatric Association. (2013). *Diagnostic and statistical manual of mental disorders* (5th ed.). Author. https://doi.org/10.1176/appi.books .9780890425596

American Psychological Association Zero Tolerance Task Force. (2008). Are zero tolerance policies effective in the schools? An evidentiary review and recommendations. *American Psychologist, 63*(9), 852–862. https://doi.org/ 10.1037/0003-066X.63.9.852

Anda, R. F., Butchart, A., Felitti, V. J., & Brown, D. W. (2010). Building a framework for global surveillance of the public health implications of adverse childhood experiences. *American Journal of Preventive Medicine, 39*(1), 93–98. https://doi.org/10.1016/j.amepre.2010.03.015

Bailey, K. (2019). *Some days I flip my lid.* PESI Publishing & Media.

Balfanz, R., Byrnes, V., & Fox, J. (2014). Sent home and put off-track: The antecedents, disproportionalities, and consequences of being suspended in the 9th grade. *Journal of Applied Research on Children: Informing Policy for Children at Risk, 5*(2), 1–18. http://digitalcommons.library.tmc.edu/ childrenatrisk/vol5/iss2/13

Bandura, A., Barbaranelli, C., Caprara, G., & Pastorelli, C. (1996). Multifaceted impact of self-efficacy beliefs on academic functioning. *Child Development, 67*(3), 1206–1222.

Barron, I., & Abdallah, G. (2015). Intergenerational trauma in the occupied Palestinian territories: Effect on children and promotion of healing. *Journal of Child & Adolescent Trauma, 8,* 103–110. https://doi.org/10.1007/ s40653-015-0046-z

Blodgett, C. (2015, March). *No school alone: How community risks and assets contribute to school and youth success.* Washington State University. https://erdc.wa.gov/publications-and-reports/no-school-alone-how-community-risks-and-assets-contribute-to-school-and-youth-success

Blum, R. W. (2005). A case for school connectedness. *Educational Leadership, 62*(7), 16–20.

Bowlby, J. (1982). *Attachment and loss, Vol. 1: Attachment* (2nd ed.). Basic Books.

Bowlby, J., May, D. S., & Solomon, M. F. (1989). *Attachment separation & loss* [Video]. Continuing Education Seminars.

Brady, K., Forton, M., & Porter, D. (2015). *Rules in school: Teaching discipline in the classroom.* The Center for Responsive Schools.

Brendtro, L. K., Brokenleg, M., & Van Bockern, S. (2014). Environments where children thrive: The circle of courage model. *Reclaiming Children and Youth, 23*(3), 10.

Bruning, R., Dempsey, M., Kauffman, D. F., McKim, C., & Zumbrunn, S. (2013). Examining dimensions of self-efficacy for writing. *Journal of Educational Psychology, 105*(1), 25–38. https://doi.org/10.1037/A0029692

Cannon, B. (1994). Walter Bradford Cannon: Reflections on the man and his contributions. *International Journal of Stress Management, 1*(2), 145–158.

Cook, A., Spinazzola, J., Ford, J., Lanktree, C., Blaustein, M., Cloitre, M., De Rosa, R., Hubbard, R., Kagan, R., Liautaud, J., Mallah, K., Olafson, E., & van der Kolk, B. (2005). Complex trauma in children and adolescents. *Psychiatric Annals, 35*(5), 390–398. https://doi.org/10.3928/00485713-20050501-05

Duke, N. N., Pettingell, S. L., McMorris, B. J., & Borowski, I. W. (2010). Associations with mulitple types of adverse childhood experiences. *Pediatrics, 125*(4), 778–786. https://doi.org/10.1542/peds.2009-0597

Education for All Handicapped Children Act, Pub.L. 94-142. (1975). https://www.govinfo.gov/content/pkg/STATUTE-89/pdf/STATUTE-89-Pg773.pdf

Enlow, M. B., Egeland, B., Blood, E. A., Wright, R. O., & Wright, R. J. (2012). Interpersonal trauma exposure and cognitive development in children to age 8 years: A longitudinal study. *Journal of Epidemiology and Community Health, 66*(11), 1005–1010. https://doi.org/10.1136/jech-2011-200727

Greene, R. W. (2018). Transforming school discipline: Shifting from power and control to collaboration and problem solving. *Childhood Education, 94*(4), 22–27. https://doi.org/10.1080/00094056.2018.1494430

Hanson, J. L., Nacewicz, B. M., Sutterer, M. J., Cayo, A. A., Schaefer, S. M., Rudolph, K. D., Shirtcliff, E. A., Pollak, S. D., & Davidson, R. J. (2014, May 22). Behavioral problems after early life stress: Contributions of the hippocampus and amygdala. *Biological Psychiatry, 77*(4), 314–323. https://doi.org/10.1016/j.biopsych.2014.04.020

The Hawn Foundation. (2011). *The MindUP Curriculum.* Author.

Individuals with Disabilities Education Act, 20 U.S.C. § 1400 (2004).

Kaplan, I., Stolk, Y., Valibhoy, M., Tucker, A., & Baker, J. (2016, February). Cognitive assessment of refugee children: Effects of trauma and new language acquisition. *Transcultural Psychiatry, 53*(1), 81–109. https://doi.org/10.1177/1363461515612933

Kunjufu, J. (2005). *Keeping black boys out of special education* (1st ed.). African American Images.

Lanier, P. (2020, July 2). *Racism is an adverse childhood experience*. The Jordan Institute for Families. https://jordaninstituteforfamilies.org/2020/racism-is-an-adverse-childhood-experience-ace/

López, L., & Páez, M. (2020). *Teaching dual language learners: What early childhood educators need to know*. Brookes Publishing.

Losen, D., Hodson, C., Keith II, M. A., Morrison, K., & Belway, S. (2015). *Are we closing the school discipline gap?* University of California. Los Angeles. http://escholarship.org/uc/item/2t36g571

Lovallo, W. R. (2013, October). Early life adversity reduces stress reactivity and impulsive behavior: Implications for health behaviors. *International Journal of Psychophysiology, 90*, 8–16.

Lovorn, M. G. (2008). Humor in the home and in the classroom: The benefits of laughing while we learn. *Journal of Education and Human Development, 2*(1).

Lutz, F., Reynolds, C., & Kamphaus, R. (2004). *Behavior rating inventory of executive function* (2nd ed.). PAR.

Mackrain, M. (2013). *Devereux adult resilience survey (DARS): An introduction*. https://centerforresilientchildren.org/wp-content/uploads/DARS-w.-BYB-sample-strategies.pdf

Medley, M. (2012, February 27). A role for English language teachers in trauma healing. *TESOL Journal, 3*(1), 110–125. https://doi.org/10.1002/tesj.6

Merritt, D. H., & Klein, S. (2015, January). Do early care and education services improve language development for maltreated children? Evidence from a national child welfare sample. *Child Abuse & Neglect, 39*, 185–196. http://dx.doi.org/10.1016/j.chiabu.2014.10.011

Moses, L., Rylak, D., Reader, T., Hertz, C., & Ogden, M. (2020). Educators' perspectives on supporting student agency. *Theory Into Practice, 59*(2), 213–222.

Neuhoff, C. C., & Schaefer, C. (2002). Effects of laughing, smiling, and howling on mood. *Psychological Reports, 91*(3_suppl), 1079–1080.

PACEs Connection. (2020, October 6). *3 realms of ACEs*. https://www.pacesconnection.com/blog/3-realms-of-aces-updated

Perkins, S. C., Finegood, E. D., & Swain, J. E. (2013, April). Poverty and language development: Roles of parenting and stress. *Innovations in clinical neuroscience, 10*(4), 10–19.

Phifer, L. W., & Hull, R. (2016). Helping students heal: Observations of trauma-informed practices in the schools. *School Mental Health, 8*(1), 201–205. https://doi.org/10.1007/s12310-016-9183-2

Porges, S. W., & Carter, C. S. (2017). Polyvagal theory and the social engagement system. In P. L. Gerbarg, P. R. Muskin, & R. P. Brown (Eds.), *Complementary and integrative treatments in psychiatric practice* (pp. 221–236). American Psychiatric Publishing.

Reynolds, C. R., & Kamphaus, R. W. (2015). BASC-3: *Behavior assessment system for children* (3rd ed.). Pearson.

Rosenthal, D. A., Gurney, R. M., & Moore, S. M. (1981). From trust to inti-macy: A new inventory for examining Erikson's stages of psychosocial development. *Journal of Youth and Adolescence, 10*(6), 525–537. https://doi .org/10.1007/BF02087944

Rowan, R., Mustaoha, M., Jung, P., Hindocha, C., Bisby, J., & Bloomfield, M. (2020). The effects of developmental trauma on reinforcement learning and its relationship to psychotic experiences: A behavioural study. *BMJ Yale.* https://www.medrxiv.org/content/10.1101/2020.11.18.20234112v1

Ryan, T. G., & Goodram, B. (2013). The impact of exclusionary discipline on stu-dents. *International Journal of Progressive Education, 9*(3), 169–177. https:// ijpe.inased.org/makale/2463

Schore, A. N. (2009). Relational trauma and the developing right brain: The neu-robiology of broken attachment bonds. In T. Baradon (Ed.), *Relational trauma in infancy: Psychoanalytic, attachment and neuropsychological contributions to parent–infant psychotherapy* (pp. 19–47). Routledge/Taylor & Francis Group.

Schrank, F. A., & Wendling, B. J. (2018). The Woodcock–Johnson IV: Tests of cog-nitive abilities, tests of oral language, tests of achievement. In D. P. Flana-gan & E. M. McDonough (Eds.), *Contemporary intellectual assessment: Theories, tests, and issues* (pp. 383–451). Guilford.

Sege, R. D. & Brown, C. H. (2017). Responding to ACEs with HOPE: Health out-comes from positive experiences. *Academic Pediatrics, 17*(7S), S79–S85.

Siegel, D. J. (2012). *The developing mind: how relationships and the brain interact to shape who we are* (2nd ed). Guilford.

Skiba, R. J., Chung, C., Trachok, M., Baker, T. L., Sheya, A., & Hughes, R. L. (2014). Parsing disciplinary disproportionality: Contributions of infrac-tion, student, and school characteristics to out-of-school suspension and expulsion. *American Education Research Journal, 51*(4), 640–670. https://doi .org/10.3102/0002831214541670

Skinner, B. F. (1974). *About behaviorism.* Knopf.

Skinner, M. E., & Hales, M. R. (1992). Classroom teachers' "explanations" of student behavior: One possible barrier to the acceptance and use of applied behav-ior analysis procedures in the schools. *Journal of Educational & Psychological Consultation, 3*(3), 219–232. https://doi.org/10.1207/s1532768xjepc0303_2

Solomon, J. C. (1996). Humor and aging well: a laughing matter or a matter of laughing? *American Behavioral Scientist, 39*(3), 249–271.

Strosnider, R., & Sharpe, V. (2019). *The executive function guidebook: Strategies to help all students achieve success.* Corwin.

Substance Abuse and Mental Health Services Administration (SAMHSA). (2014). *SAMHSA's concept of trauma and guidance for a trauma-informed approach.* HHS Publication No. (SMA) 14-4884. Substance Abuse and Mental Health Services Administration. https://store.samhsa.gov/product/SAMHSA-s-Concept-of-Trauma-and-Guidance-for-a-Trauma-Informed-Approach/ SMA14-4884

Tomlinson, C. A. (2017). *How to differentiate instruction in academically diverse class-rooms* (3rd ed.). ASCD.

Tottenham, N., & Sheridan, M. A. (2010). A review of adversity, the amygdala and the hippocampus: a consideration of developmental timing. *Frontiers In Human Neuroscience, 368.* https://doi.org/10.3389/neuro.09.068.2009

van der Kolk, B. A. (2005). Developmental trauma disorder: Toward a rational diagnosis for children with complex trauma histories. *Psychiatric Annals, 35*(5), 401–409.

van der Kolk, B. A., Pynoos, R. S., Cichetti, D., Cloitre, M., Putnam, F.W., Saxe, G., Spinazzola, J., Stolbach, B. C., & Teicher, M. (2009, February 1). *Proposal to include developmental trauma disorder diagnosis for children and adolescents in DSM-V.* http://www.cttntraumatraining.org/uploads/4/6/2/3/46231093/dsm-v_proposal-dtd_taskforce.pdf

Verschueren, K., Marcoen, A., & Schoefs, V. (1996). The internal working model of the self, attachment, and competence in five-year-olds. *Child Development, 67*(5), 2493–2511. https://doi.org/10.2307/1131636

Wechsler, D. (2014). *WISC-V: Wechsler intelligence scale for children.* NCS Pearson, Inc.

Wechsler, D. (2020). *WIAT-4: Wechsler individual achievement test* (4th ed.). Pearson.

Williams, P. (2017). Student agency for powerful learning. *Knowledge Quest, 45*(4), 9–16.

Zolkoski, S. M., & Bullock, L. M. (2012). Resilience in children and youth: A review. *Children and Youth Services Review, 34*(12), 2295–2303. https://doi.org/10.1016/j.childyouth.2012.08.009

Index

The letter *f* following a page number denotes a figure.

About the Author

Melissa Sadin, EdD, is the executive director of Ducks & Lions: Trauma Sensitive Resources and the director of special services at Unity Charter School in Morristown, New Jersey. She has served as a special education teacher, a gifted education teacher, and a building administrator. Most recently, she served as a director of special education.

Sadin has been vice president of her local school board and is recognized as a Master School Board Member. She has conducted research on the perceptions of teachers working to create trauma-informed classrooms and is a published author and has produced numerous webinars on children with attachment trauma in schools. Currently, Sadin works as a director of exceptional education and as an education consultant and developmental trauma expert providing professional development to school districts, municipal service providers, and parents. Nationally, she is a highly sought after keynote speaker and conference presenter. Her Trauma Guide Series of books is available on her website at www.traumasensitive.com.

Related ASCD Resources: Trauma and Special Education

At the time of publication, the following resources were available (ASCD stock numbers in parentheses).

Building on the Strengths of Students with Special Needs: How to Move Beyond Disability Labels in the Classroom by Toby J. Karten (#117023)

Co-Planning for Co-Teaching: Time-Saving Routines That Work in Inclusive Classrooms (ASCD Arias) by Gloria Lodato Wilson (#117018)

Creating a Trauma-Sensitive Classroom (QRG) by Kristin Souers and Pete Hall (#QRG118054)

Decoding Autism and Leading the Way to Successful Inclusion by Barbara Boroson (#118008)

Fostering Resilient Learners: Strategies for Creating a Trauma-Sensitive Classroom by Kristin Souers with Pete Hall (#116014)

From Goals to Growth: Intervention and Support in Every Classroom by Lee Ann Jung (#118032)

Inclusion Dos, Don'ts, and Do Betters (QRG) by Toby Karten (#QRG116082)

Leading an Inclusive School: Access and Success for ALL Students by Richard A. Villa and Jacqueline S. Thousand (#116022)

Relationship, Responsibility, and Regulation: Trauma-Invested Practices for Fostering Resilient Learners by Kristin Souers with Pete Hall (#119027)

Restoring Students' Innate Power: Trauma-Responsive Strategies for Teaching Multilingual Newcomers by Louise El Yaafouri (#122004)

Success with IEPs: Solving Five Common Implementation Challenges in the Classroom (ASCD Arias) by Vicki Caruana (#117047)

A Teacher's Guide to Special Education by David F. Bateman and Jenifer L. Cline (#116019)

Teaching to Strengths: Supporting Students Living with Trauma, Violence, and Chronic Stress by Debbie Zacarian, Lourdes Alvarez-Ortiz, and Judie Haynes (#117035)

Trauma-Invested Practices to Meet Students' Needs (QRG) by Kristin Souers and Pete Hall (#QRG119077)

Trauma-Sensitive School Leadership: Building a Learning Environment to Support Healing and Success by Bill Ziegler, Dave Ramage, and Andrea Parson (#122013)

Your Students, My Students, Our Students: Rethinking Equitable and Inclusive Classrooms by Lee Ann Jung, Nancy Frey, Douglas Fisher and Julie Kroener (#119019)

For up-to-date information about ASCD resources, go to **www.ascd.org**. You can search the complete archives of *Educational Leadership* at **www.ascd.org/el**. To contact us, send an email to **member@ascd.org** or call 1-800-933-2723 or 703-578-9600.

ascd
whole child

The ASCD Whole Child approach is an effort to transition from a focus on narrowly defined academic achievement to one that promotes the long-term development and success of all children. Through this approach, ASCD supports educators, families, community members, and policymakers as they move from a vision about educating the whole child to sustainable, collaborative actions.

Trauma-Informed Teaching and IEPs relates to all five of the whole child tenets.

For more about the ASCD Whole Child approach,
visit **www.ascd.org/wholechild.**

WHOLE CHILD
TENETS

1 HEALTHY
Each student enters school healthy and learns about and practices a healthy lifestyle.

2 SAFE
Each student learns in an environment that is physically and emotionally safe for students and adults.

3 ENGAGED
Each student is actively engaged in learning and is connected to the school and broader community.

4 SUPPORTED
Each student has access to personalized learning and is supported by qualified, caring adults.

5 CHALLENGED
Each student is challenged academically and prepared for success in college or further study and for employment and participation in a global environment.